Reputation
Risk
Management

Reputation
Risk
Management

PETER SHELDON GREEN

FINANCIAL TIMES

PITMAN PUBLISHING

Pitman Publishing
128 Long Acre, London WC2E 9AN

A Division of Longman Group UK Limited

First published in 1992

© Longman Group UK Limited 1992

British Library Cataloguing in Publication Data
A CIP catalogue record for this book can be obtained from the British
Library

ISBN 0 273 03869 9

Phototypeset in Linotron Times Roman
by Northern Phototypesetting Co. Ltd., Bolton
Printed and bound in Great Britain
by Biddles Ltd., Guildford

For Mrs Angela Perry,
with thanks for everything

CONTENTS

    'At the coalface' – The Cambridge Vet School campaign
    Lindy Beveridge   114

16 EQUIPMENT FOR CRISIS MANAGEMENT   117

17 INFORMATION AND DECISION AIDS   122
    'At the coalface' – Product recalls   *Peter Gavan*   126

18 MEDIA RELATIONS IN CRISIS   131

19 RESEARCH AND FEEDBACK   137

20 TESTING AND TRAINING FOR CRISIS   140
    'At the coalface' – Tests, trials and tribulations
    William Comery   148

21 THE ROLE OF CONSULTANTS   156

22 LAWYERS AND OTHER EXPERTS   160
    'At the coalface' – Crisis planning: common sense or
    defeatism?   *Charles Griffith*   165

23 ADVERTISING   168

24 THE CULPABLE COMPANY   171

25 RRM AS THE COMPANY CONSCIENCE   177

26 PUTTING IT ALL TOGETHER   181

    Appendix   186

    Index   200

PREFACE

This book has been written against a background of increased awareness of the level of risks which a company can face due to disasters, malicious action and errors on its own part. The wide publicity which has been given to such events has brought the whole question of crisis management very much more to the fore amongst management skills. With this increased awareness of the need for crisis management has come a realisation that such a programme cannot be confined to crisis alone and needs to be a continuing discipline in relation to the important area of company reputation.

In writing this book I have drawn heavily on direct experience of establishing and administering reputation risk management and crisis management programmes. I have also drawn greatly on the views and knowledge of other experts working in the field, too numerous to mention by name but some, at least, credited within the text of the book. Special thanks are due to my colleagues at Sheldon Communications and in particular to Ms Hillary Box whose inputs have been invaluable particularly in clarifying the theoretical basis of the opening chapters of the book and Ms Karen Kelly for her work in researching information.

Reputation Risk Management is a relatively new management discipline and much of the terminology used is still being invented. Many of the issues and techniques discussed in the book may be familiar under different names – the book itself is, I hope, about content rather than labels.

I should make one brief point about style. Where it has been excessively clumsy to use the term 'he or she' for the third person pronoun I have, rather reluctantly, adopted the masculine form as the more gender-neutral alternative. In doing so I have followed convention but have no wish to suggest any form of gender preference in management roles.

INTRODUCTION

Any business which failed to take steps to protect its assets would normally be regarded as incompetently managed. It would be a very strange business indeed which did not ensure reasonable protection against fire, theft, vandalism etc., and which did not in addition take out insurance to provide cover in case the precautions which had been taken failed. The business which failed to protect those balance sheet assets which are represented by debtors through a system of credit control, and possibly credit insurance, would be treading a perilous path. Yet there is a very real asset of most established businesses which seems to be offered very little protection in far too many cases.

The asset which we may call 'reputation' accounts for a significant part of the difference between the book value of a business and its market worth. It surfaces as 'brand value' or as 'goodwill' and it can often be the single most valuable asset which a business owns. Very considerable sums of money may be spent in creating reputation and in establishing ownership and benefit from such reputation. Yet the discipline of formally defending this asset against risk remains in its infancy.

There is no reason why reputation should not be treated like any other asset and a formal programme implemented to provide reputation risk management as a continuing discipline aimed at protecting reputation against threat, wherever this may come from. Of course an increasing number of companies are developing reputation risk management programmes and a great number more have fragments of such a programme in place frequently under the title of 'crisis management'. A surprising number of businesses, however, have no continuing programme, no standing plan to handle the external relations aspects of a crisis should it occur, and little understanding that such omissions allow a major asset to be unnecessarily at risk.

In recent years 'crisis management' has become a fashionable term particularly in the communications business and has become a lucrative addition to the portfolios of PR firms and a variety of other consultants. There can be no question that it has value – one only has to consider the number of times a controllable problem has been blown up into a disaster by ill-considered management comment and action to see the consequences of ignoring the skills of crisis management. But in itself crisis management is not enough to provide a proper programme for reputation. It is a last ditch technique, resorted to when all else fails and, all too often, has to be grafted on to an organisational structure which is neither prepared nor equipped to perform properly in the sort of crisis situation implied. Without a full programme of reputation risk management problems become crises and crises become vastly more difficult to manage than they need to be.

Of course such a programme is, in essence, a form of insurance. It is self insurance and it does not offer full compensation but only damage limitation. It involves investing time and money which one sincerely hopes will be largely wasted. This is no argument for not making the investment, however, any more than it is an argument against any other form of insurance or protection for any other form of asset.

It is possible to take out insurance for the very specific type of crisis of consumer terrorism and this insurance does cover re-establishing the reputation of the brand. At the time of writing only two Lloyds Underwriters offer this and, understandably, names of companies carrying such insurance are confidential. It is expensive and largely unproven and falls outside the main arguments of this book, but serves as a further reminder that it is not exclusively marketing men and some accountants who recognise the value of reputation.

The purpose of this book is to examine the considerations which need to be taken into account when looking at a reputation risk management programme and to provide a practical set of guidelines for establishing such a programme.

In industry there remains a degree of resistance to investing significant time and money in reputation risk management programmes and one's experience is that, even when such an investment has been made, the level of management commitment and the size of allocated budget is often unrealistically limited. The somewhat proselytising tone of some of the earlier chapters is, perhaps, a reaction to such attitudes and may strike a chord with those professionals who are involved in reputation risk and crisis management on a regular basis.

Throughout the book I have attempted to follow a logical progression which moves from the arguments for setting up a reputation risk management programme, through the budgeting and structure of such a programme, on to the broad principles of the day-to-day operation of the programme and then to a discussion of the 'sharp end' of reputation risk management – crisis management. This structure has meant that there are a number of specific issues which have proved difficult to handle within the main discussion of the text. Some have been dealt with as short digressions. Other queries which, in general, are ones I have encountered during preliminary discussions with clients or as audience questions at lectures, are dealt with as a series of short chapters towards the end of the book.

Interspersed in the main text of the book are a number of case histories or personal viewpoints from people directly involved in the business of managing reputation risk. I have called these 'At the Coal Face' for obvious reasons and am most grateful to those people who have contributed or allowed their work to be discussed. Inevitably most successful, and unsuccessful, case histories are highly confidential and there are few references to companies by name. Nonetheless, it is hoped that these insights will help to illuminate and provide a context for the main body of the work.

At present the main focus of attention on reputation protection continues to be concerned with crisis management, but this is changing rapidly and most experts in the field of crisis management are already recommending and implementing programmes which run on a continuous basis and which are equipped to handle risk to reputation at what might be described as a sub-crisis level.

Skills in crisis management as a formal discipline have largely been developed by and confined to PR practitioners, both in house and, more usually, in consultancies. This is perfectly logical since the techniques used to handle the reputation element of a corporate crisis are drawn from the world of public relations. One suspects that such expertise will not long stay confined to PR people, however, but will become an intrinsic part of management consultants' services and more of a general management consideration within companies.

I have little doubt that reputation risk management will become a discipline of increasing importance to companies as threats to reputation multiply and as there is increased awareness of the value which should be placed on reputation. Already very considerable sums of money are spent in building such reputation at a corporate and at a product level. Protection of this investment is plain common sense.

1 VALUING REPUTATION

Reputation risk management is a formal structuring of those skills and techniques used to protect a company's reputation. The reputation to be protected may be that of the company itself; it may be the brands owned by the company; on occasion it may be the reputation of key individuals within the company. As a formal discipline it is a relatively new concept, though the principles behind it and many of the techniques employed are far from new.

The element of reputation risk management known as 'crisis management' has become widely recognised in recent years and tends to be viewed as a complete management operation in its own right. In practice, the need to employ crisis management techniques is, more often than not, an indication that reputation risk management has not been implemented – or that the programme has failed.

It has been said that war is diplomacy carried on by other means. Crisis management has the same relationship to reputation risk management. Both war and crisis management are final, undesirable and often avoidable expedients. Both war and crisis management suggest that diplomatic or reputation risk management measures have been circumvented, or have been ineffective.

WHAT PRICE REPUTATION?

Reputation risk management is concerned with asset protection. The asset involved is in the form of reputation. An essential first step to instituting a programme designed to protect this asset is to formulate some idea of what reputation is worth. Until a price tag can be put on a reputation, it is impossible to assess accurately whether it is worth 'insuring' through a reputation risk management programme. At first sight this would appear to be a daunting task but fortunately it is not something which we have to consider from scratch. We can start by looking at the potentially huge but intangible asset represented by brands.

Brand valuation

There has been a long and sometimes acrimonious debate over whether or not companies should place a value on their brands and include this value in their balance sheet. (In this context, 'brands' applies to services just as much as to products.)

Grand Met have been allocating a balance sheet figure for the value of their brands since 1988. Rank Hovis McDougall, despite an initial reluctance, fairly rapidly followed suit. On the other hand many companies who own powerful international brands have absolutely no intention of putting a balance sheet value on them.

The debate is about accountancy practice and it is an extremely complicated one. There is, however, no debate about the underlying assumption that brands have a real value. Indeed there is widespread understanding that brands are often a company's major asset, whether or not included in its book valuation.

Valuing brands, or attempting to place a proper value on brands, has become an industry in its own right and the arguments for and against showing them as balance sheet assets have become wide ranging. Placing a value on brands can significantly increase the declared assets of a company – providing protection against takeover and making fund raising easier. In Britain the Accounting Standards Committee says a brand value should be written off against profits over a 20 to 40 year period. In practice, this may be nonsensical. A brand may increase hugely in value over such a period and amortising its value could be as inappropriate as progressively writing down the value of the Van Gogh oil painting which hangs in the board room.

The purchase of Rowntree Mackintosh by the Swiss food group Nestlé for £2.55 billion in 1988 clearly demonstrates just how valuable brand reputation may be seen to be. Rowntree's physical assets in the form of plant and stock accounted for one-fifth of the purchase price. The remaining four-fifths of Nestlé's money went to pay for Rowntree's marketing know-how and infrastructure and for its reputation in the form of a fine traditional corporate image and major brand names. And this is far from a one off example. In precisely the same way, when Phillip Morris bought Kraft for $12.9 million at around the same time, the price paid was four times the value of tangible assets. Both of these deals were carried out in the late 1980s when the value placed on brands was at a particularly high point. But they show quite emphatically just how valuable hard-headed money men believe reputation to be.

Of course, none of this is really new. In a fairly informal way it has always been known that an element of the value of virtually every business lies in its reputation, whether that reputation relates to a company itself or to its various services and products. This reputation value is to be found in the smallest successful business. The 'goodwill' element negotiated in the purchase price of a corner shop or a café is precisely the same element as the corporate and brand reputations paid for in the Nestlé/Rowntree mega-deal.

In reality business has been placing a value on goodwill since trade began. The practice of 'buying the brand' did not start with IBM computers. It did not even start with Coca Cola. It probably started with trade in flint tools when a known craftsman's skills were sufficient to ensure that his mark on a tool automatically increased its value. Thus an arrowhead from Og was worth half as many rabbit skins again as one from Ig, and once Og's reputation was established, the difference was as much in that reputation as in the arrowhead itself.

So it is already the case that reputation is known to have value and the debate about brand valuation and balance sheet assets has done no more than to focus attention on something of which everyone in business was already aware. But this focusing of attention is important, and not only to accountants and financiers. By reminding everyone that reputation has value and that this value is, in principle at least, formally expressible in terms of money, the debate on brands has brought timely attention to the fact that a company's reputation is a genuine asset. Like any other asset it needs maintaining and developing. Like any other asset it makes sense to insure it as far as is practically possible.

CALCULATING THE RRM PREMIUM

If we can place a value on reputation, then we should begin to introduce some sort of discipline to our attitude towards how much we should be prepared to invest in terms of time and money towards protection of this reputation. When protecting the physical assets of a business, the amount to be spent on security systems, fire protection and the like is largely determined by two factors – the value of the assets involved and the degree of risk involved. The level of insurance cover and cost of premiums are determined by similar yardsticks. In the case of the intangible asset of reputation we similarly need to have some idea of its value and of risk levels.

Valuing the reputation asset

When we look at the examples of the Nestlé/Rowntree and the Phillip Morris/Kraft takeovers it becomes apparent that values placed on reputation can be very high indeed. This is confirmed by the sort of values placed on brands by those companies which follow this accounting practice. In 1991, for example, Cadbury announced an addition of £309 million to its balance sheet to cover acquisitions made since 1985 including the Trebor and Bassett brands. Most significantly, the company said it would not be amortising this figure.

It would be simplistic to equate brand value totally with either reputation, customer esteem or consumer awareness since this would not reflect commercial reality. (In fact, brand valuation for balance sheet purposes is an extremely skilled and complex activity.) But it would be accurate to say that, should the reputation of a brand be totally destroyed, then so would the brand value. In the context of reputation risk management, therefore, the assumed asset value of reputation to be protected can indeed be equated with the brand value. The argument that, for the purpose of protecting reputation, the value of a brand's reputation actually equates to the value of the brand itself, can be summarised as:

1 Reputation, though not the only consideration, is a necessary condition for a brand to have value.
2 Therefore, if a brand's reputation is lost, the necessary conditions for value fail to be met.
3 Thus the destruction of a brand's reputation is equivalent to the destruction of a brand's value.

(For a discussion of the issues raised and the techniques employed in brand valuation by perhaps the leading exponent in this field see Appendix 1.)

For the purposes of assessing appropriate risk management 'insurance cover' levels for a brand, we simply ask: 'What is the realistic price for which the brand, excluding stocks and production facilities, could be sold to a willing buyer?' i.e.

RISK REPUTATION COVER (PRODUCTS)

Buyer's price minus stock and production facilities

What is true for brands is equally true for companies as a whole. The value of a business can be determined by a whole series of criteria including book value of assets, past record of profitability, forward order book and, possibly, 'goodwill'. One might think that 'goodwill' should be the only reputation element in such a valuation. But what price past trading record or forward order book if a company's reputation is destroyed or significantly damaged? Just as with brands, the destruction of a business's reputation may be regarded, in the context of risk reputation assessment, as equivalent to the destruction of the greater part of that business' value.

To assess the risk management cover that should be allowed for companies, we would subtract the value of physical assets and 'know-how' (such as customer contacts, staff sales skills, marketing intelligence held by the company) from the buyer's price.

RISK REPUTATION COVER (COMPANIES)

Buyer's price minus physical assets and know-how

Assessing the risks

In addition to looking at the value of reputation we also need to have some measure of how seriously it may be at risk before considering what, if any, steps need to be taken to protect it. Assessing the degree to which reputation may be at risk is, perhaps, less straightforward than valuation. Nevertheless, it is an exercise that must be undertaken – and reviewed regularly – in an effective risk management programme. The complexities of this area are discussed in detail in Chapter 3, which also gives a series of guidelines for risk assessment. At this point it is sufficient to say that anyone who has witnessed in recent years the damage done to brands, product groups and companies by events ranging from product tampering to health scares, and from natural disasters to ill-considered comment, can have little doubt that the risks are very real.

An important factor in looking at risks to reputation is that it is as much a matter of perception as it is of real events. The premium value of Og's flint arrowheads will drop as soon as his sight starts to fail. But it will also drop if a rumour goes around the caves that his sight is failing, even if his eyes are as good as ever.

In today's world a claim by, let us say, the Animal Liberation Front to have poisoned a certain brand of food product has the potential to stop sales dead – even if the claim is false. The fact that this technique of the 'false threat' is being used increasingly by blackmailers is evidence of its success. In some instances, the fact that food products have not been tampered with has even given some blackmailers a dubious moral cachet. A fine example of extremely poor risk management for the companies and products involved.

Reputation can suffer both short- and long-term damage and protection is needed against both. Even if reputation can be fully restored this may take time and the eventual total rehabilitation of the asset value of reputation does not compensate for lost sales while this process is taking place. For some businesses the recovery period may be simply too long and companies go under before reputation can be rebuilt.

SUMMARY

These twin themes – that reputation has value and that reputation is at risk – will be returned to time and again in this book. Pinning down the value represented by reputation and making an accurate assessment of the spread and severity of risk provides a means to considering reputation risk management in a quantifiable way and, in doing so, gives us a yardstick against which to measure the importance of this discipline.

A further recurring theme will be that reputation is a peculiarly vulnerable asset and that any reputation risk management programme needs to take this into account, both in terms of what steps need to be taken to prevent risk developing into reality, and what steps need to be taken to limit damage when the unavoidable crisis occurs.

Summary points

- Reputation risk management – the formal structuring of skills and techniques to protect reputation.
- Reputation has monetary value and should be 'insured' against risk through the reputation risk management programme.
- Reputation 'premiums' are calculated by:
  – assessing the monetary value of reputation;
  – assessing the level of risk.

2 REPUTATION = PUBLIC PERCEPTION

It is clear that reputation has a value in itself and that the worth which can be placed on reputation is peculiarly vulnerable to rapid devaluation. It should also be obvious that this devaluation may come about as a result of events or actions which are totally outside the immediate control of the owner of that reputation.

HERE TODAY – GONE TOMORROW?

The impact on British egg producers of Edwina Currie's comments on salmonella in eggs has passed into folk lore – both political and commercial. A warning on the danger to the elderly, the sick and the pregnant of listeria in soft cheeses from the Government's Health Officer had a similarly devastating short-term effect on the sales of soft French cheeses in the UK. In both these instances, public comment combined with a high degree of media hype to destroy, at least temporarily, the reputation of these two product groups.

In the case of eggs some steps have been taken to reduce the incidence of salmonella by imposing controls on foodstuffs and conditions at the battery farms. In the case of soft cheeses nothing has been done, because there was never any need to. For both British eggs and French soft cheeses UK sales did eventually revert to their pre-panic levels, but in neither instance was this achieved without considerable effort and investment having been made to rebuild lost reputation.

Of course, reputation can be built as well as destroyed by factors which are not intrinsically a part of the brand, service or company in themselves. Successful advertising, skilled public relations, good packaging, imaginative sponsorships, promotions and point of sale materials are just some of the ways in which investment is made when building and then maintaining a reputation. Reputation is usually built over a number of years at very considerable expense. Rebuilding may be even more costly.

PERCEPTIONS v. REALITIES

One of the most interesting, and widely publicised, cases of rebuilding reputation was in the case of the American brand of painkiller 'Tylenol'. This is a classic case history and we will come back to it more than once during the course of this book. The facts of what happened to 'Tylenol' are fairly straightforward and well documented.

On 30 September, 1982 three people in the Chicago area of the USA died as a result of taking 'Tylenol' capsules which had been poisoned with cyanide. This poisoning was in no way the fault of the product's manufacturers, Johnson and Johnson, and did not happen within the factory. These initial deaths were followed by a further three fatalities and by a 'copy-cat' killing where a different poison was used. As a result, Johnson and Johnson, acting in full consultation with the FBI, withdrew 'Tylenol' capsules temporarily from the market (at a cost of some US$ 100 million). 'Tylenol' had, at the time of the poisonings, a 35% share of the US painkiller market and annual sales of US$400 million.

Public faith in the 'Tylenol' brand, in tablets which had not been poisoned, as well in as the capsule formulation which had, and, to some extent, public faith in the huge Johnson and Johnson empire itself was shattered. On Wall Street there was a 20% fall in the company's share price – reducing the company's value by US$2 billion. The massive publicity which attended these events and the very real public disquiet which resulted made it seem as if 'Tylenol' was finished as a brand. Indeed, much informed market opinion at the time believed that the best course for Johnson and Johnson was to launch a new, differently named brand to take up the slack in the market. The fact that the company chose not to do this but instead successfully rebuilt the 'Tylenol' brand is a superb example of successful crisis management. How they did it is discussed later. The point under discussion here is why they did it.

Johnson and Johnson's Chief Executive said at the time that he recognised the fact that the reputation of 'Tylenol' was a major corporate asset, and it was an asset which he was prepared to go to huge lengths to save.

In practice the only active ingredient in 'Tylenol' is a readily available analgesic which is the basis of a number of competitive products and which is available at a much lower cost as a generic formulation. The uniqueness of 'Tylenol', which enabled it to capture more than a third of the entire US pain killer market, was in the marketing of the product. The value of the 'Tylenol' brand was a function of public perception and public perception only – not of the uniqueness of the product itself. In taking a decision to rebuild the

'Tylenol' brand, the company took a decision which related directly to the value of the brand's reputation, not to the intrinsic value of the product itself; not to the uniqueness or even superiority of the product's qualities and not to its value for money performance. (The same active ingredient was available more cheaply.)

In the case of British eggs, French soft cheeses and the proprietary brand 'Tylenol' the conclusion is the same.

Reputation value is a direct function of the perceptions of the public involved with a company or its brands. It is only contingently related to the quality of products, services or corporate performance.

In these three examples, the 'public' with whom reputation was at risk was the national consumer. It should be understood, however, that in the broader context of risk reputation, 'public' could also refer to a number of very different audiences. Had 'Tylenol' been a prescription product, for instance, the threat to perception of its reputation would have centred on the medical profession. For a manufacturing company facing rumours about plans to cease trading, its perceived reputation is at risk with its own workforce and suppliers, possibly within the local community where it is a major employer and, if it is a public company, with shareholders.

CONTROLLING PERCEPTIONS OF RISK

In the three cases cited above, the intensity of the crises faced by the producers was greatly exacerbated by a great deal of misunderstanding and false information which circulated at the time.

Salmonella was perceived to be much wider spread in eggs than was, in fact, the case. Everyone seemed to miss the fact that the listeria in cheese warning was intended only for the very vulnerable and that, again, incidence was not widespread. (This, despite the fact that the very specific groups at risk were clearly spelled out within the original Government statement.) The American public widely believed that 'Tylenol' had been poisoned in the factory, was a nationwide problem and affected tablets as well as capsules – none of which was true. Public perceptions did not correspond with reality. But, since it is public perception which determines reputation, reality can become somewhat irrelevant if enough misinformation is circulating. Planning and determination are needed to ensure that this does not happen, and even then they are not always successful unless properly managed and coordinated.

Reputation risk management is concerned with ensuring that false perceptions do not arise and with preventing an escalation into the realms of fantasy where there are real grounds for negative perceptions.

Quite clearly reputation risk management programmes cannot simply be switched on when there is a problem which already seems to be getting out of hand. It is a matter of creating a strategic programme, setting up effective systems and acting on a continuous basis which heads off potential problems before they arise; and ensuring that everything is in place to control genuine problems which cannot be prevented. In this respect, reputation risk management may be seen as parallel to normal quality control and safety measures, with the twin concerns of monitoring and acting to prevent things going wrong; and of acting fast and effectively to put things right when, inevitably, they do.

It would be absurd to suggest that reputation risk management will stop any event occurring which places reputation at risk. It is sometimes suggested that any reputation crisis should be avoidable. Quite clearly there is a whole range of such disasters, from oil spills to consumer tampering, which no reputation risk management programme could prevent from happening. Conversely, there is a long list of risk areas which, if monitored and anticipated, can be avoided or headed off, including careless comments by senior executives, Government activity, issue of unpalatable news about a company and the spread of unfounded rumour. These techniques of monitoring and anticipation within a reputation risk management programme also ensure that damage is kept to a minimum when events outside the direct control of the programme precipitate a reputation crisis.

Although there may appear to be a difference between avoidable and unavoidable crises, there is a great deal of overlap in the skills and methods required in both cases. The very fact that there is a formalised programme in place offers a capability for acting in all circumstances. Such circumstances can vary widely – no two crises are quite the same and no two sets of events which, without proper management, will precipitate a crisis are quite the same.

SUMMARY

Broadly speaking, the greatest danger to an organisation's reputation is likely to result from incomplete, slanted or false information. It is simply not true to say that one gets the reputation one deserves – that is, perhaps, the best that one can hope for. Events will occur which have the potential to damage an organisation's reputation. The extent to which they do so will greatly depend on how these are perceived rather than on the events themselves. This is as true for the perceptions of a Government committee considering a piece of legislation as it is for the general public.

The failure to recognise the fundamental fact that reputation depends on perception has allowed many a manageable problem to become a serious crisis for the organisations concerned. It is the function of reputation risk management to safeguard an organisation's reputation which may have taken years to build and which can so easily, even casually, be damaged or destroyed.

Summary points

- Reputation is built on perception.
- Perception of reputation is vulnerable to real and imaginary threats; both are equally dangerous.
- Reputation risk management should:
  - identify and head off the avoidable threat;
  - control and minimise the unavoidable threat.

3 WHAT ARE THE RISKS?

Reputation can be at risk in so many varied ways that it is essential to make judgements about areas and extent of risk as a preliminary to committing to and designing a reputation risk management programme.

RISKS CHANGE

Clearly some sectors of business are more at risk than others and this level of risk can intensify or recede in line with external circumstances. For example changing public perceptions on environmental issues have significantly altered attitudes towards corporate behaviour and individual products which, in turn, has meant increased risk levels for businesses with a real or perceived exposure in these areas. Consumer environmental concerns in the last decade have had an impact on organisations ranging from multinational oil companies through toiletries and cosmetics retailers to charities.

Changing patterns of behaviour in society at large may also result in a change in the levels of risk faced, particularly in relation to the unavoidable crisis. Since the early 1980s, food companies have been seen to be particularly at risk and it is interesting to note the areas which just one company in the food industry in the UK has identified as risk areas.

The list is far from comprehensive but gives some indication of how extensive risk can be. Only brand specific risks are considered which ignores the threats which can be faced by a product within a generic group – as seen with eggs and soft cheeses previously – and which similarly ignores any corporate risks which may or may not relate to brands. (The 'Tylenol' case mentioned in the last chapter graphically demonstrates how seriously risks to a brand's reputation may also be to the company as a whole.)

The food manufacturer's included:

1 **consumer terrorism** (action by political or quasi-political group);

2 **extortion** (blackmail threats to poison products have been huge in some countries, notably Japan, and the largest known demand in the UK was for £15 million);

3 **grudge tampering** (usually by a former or existing employee and estimated to account for some 25% of consumer product incidents);

4 **copycat action** following public knowledge of previous incidents; (This happened to 'Tylenol' and has been a frequent consequence of widespread publicity for particular incidents.)

5 **fraudulent claims** made by members of the public with a view to gaining compensation; (Deliberate injury to babies by parents has happened in this context.)

6 **product deterioration** through length or condition of storage by distributor or retailer;

7 **product contamination** either during manufacture or during distribution;

8 **manufacturing fault during packaging** where packaging appears to have been tampered with but where, in fact, there has been a fault on the packaging line.

Of these eight risk areas, none is improbable. Indeed, all have actually occurred within the UK food industry over a relatively short period. Only with the last two items – faults within the manufacturing or packaging processes – could responsibility be assigned directly to the food manufacturer. All, however, place the manufacturer's reputation at considerable risk.

In other industries the list might be very different and thus assessment of risk based on different criteria. A major airline, for example, might well feel that avoiding the steady erosion of reputation resulting from poor management of flight delays should be regarded as normal operating procedure rather than an aspect of reputation risk management. However, the proper response to a major disaster, despite the statistical near certainty of one occurring sooner or later, clearly calls for the very sharpest and most sensitive of reputation risk management skills, carried out in a crisis mode.

THE RISK CHECK PROGRAMME

In an ideal world, it would be possible to purchase and run a software programme setting out all imaginable scenarios relevant to reputation risk management for every type of industry. In practice, such a programme would be impossibly long and complex. It could never be comprehensive and, since we have said the very nature of risk is that it is liable to change, the programme could never be guaranteed to be up to date. Any business will have some risks which are absolutely specific to that business and, even within a business, it is quite likely that there will be risks which are quite brand-specific. This is hardly surprising. If a brand has a unique selling proposition, and if the word 'unique' in this context means what it says, then that selling proposition can be uniquely threatened – even if the USP is no more than a unique product positioning.

Nevertheless, when trying to identify risk areas for your own business, it is essential to have a systematic approach and to put identified risks together into related groups.

Who checks?

At this point, it might be helpful to look at exactly who within an organisation should be looking at the risk check programme. Chapter 6 discusses in some detail who should run the risk management programme. Identifying risk areas is, as we shall see, the preliminary step in any such programme. It is important that the risk reputation manager be involved at this initial stage and he or she is the ideal person to coordinate the activity. However, it is also vital, particularly in larger organisations where intercompany communication is notoriously haphazard, to involve a team of people who are expert in the relevant fields. This would certainly include the individual in charge of health and safety and also senior management staff with specialist line responsibilities.

Drawing up a check list

There are some broad categories which can be set out as a starting point and an aid to thinking when looking at the potential risks faced by any business enterprise. A reasonable working list might be:

1 **natural disaster** for example, a plane crash following a lightning strike; oil well blowing following an earthquake;

2 **man-made disaster** plane crash resulting from pilot error; oil well blowing following systems failure;

   (A case such as the Aberfan disaster of 1967 could be said to have elements of both natural and man-made disaster. The precipitation of the slag heap could not have been prevented. It should not, however, have been sited near the village school.)

3 **product failure** design, manufacturing and packaging faults; often where the product has been inadequately or improperly tested and faults emerge some years after the launch;

4 **product sabotage** by users or terrorists, for fraudulent or political reasons;

5 **information leakage** either deliberate or accidental; to competitors or a wider audience;

6 **legislative risk** products and services may be banned or sales restricted; regulations on advertising and other marketing techniques may strangle creative campaigns; packaging legislation may demand a complete redesign;

7 **environmental issues** can threaten a whole industry, as well as a company and its products;

8 **health issues** of concern not only in the food industry. Covers working practices and overlaps to some extent with the health and safety function of an organisation;

9 **industrial relations** strikes and other crippling industrial action; loss of key personnel (with their skills and knowledge not only of the industry but of your company) – perhaps to competitors; disaffected employees account for a high percentage of product and systems sabotage;

10 **behaviour of high profile individuals** usually only larger organisations; unwise off the cuff remarks where the organisation is marketed on a personality cult; unacceptable behaviour – sexual scandals can occasionally turn into a bonus, fraud never;

11 **corporate/financial positioning** for example, failure to prepare or inform City investors properly; the 'knock on' effect for larger companies when one part of the business is at risk; ('Tylenol' again, and the Maxwell saga.)

12 **inaccurate media reporting** either by the malicious, the lazy or the ill-informed;

13 **government action** from the breaking off of diplomatic relations or trade agreements with countries who are your key trading partners or where you have just invested in a multi-million pound plant, to the issuing of statements on Listeria in soft cheeses;

14 **other**.

In each case, the question to be asked is:

'Can our reputation be placed at risk by events which might occur in the area of natural disasters?'

and so on through the above list of broad categories.

Whenever the answer is 'yes', you need to sit down and list the various types of risk in such a category. This is where drawing on the experience of other people within the organisation will be invaluable. It can be a chastening and even frightening experience to focus on risk in this way.

The category of 'other' is included in recognition of the fact that no list of categories can hope to be a catch all for every type of business. Although this list has proved effective in setting up a number of reputation risk management programmes, it may well not be perfect or comprehensive for you.

How often?

Having compiled such a list it is then necessary to go through it and make an assessment of how high the likelihood is of each identified risk occurring, either as a full blown crisis or, more frequently, as a potential crisis which needs managing before it develops

This is an assessment that can only be made on the basis of real knowledge of your business, your corporate culture and your industry. Market research and market intelligence available within the organisation will help in some measure to identify prevalence of past incidents and, possibly, future projections in some areas. Use these resources fully but be aware that they can only be guidelines and that a certain amount of intelligent guess work will be necessary. The only practical advice to give here is to adopt a 'worst possible' assessment. The adage 'If the worst can happen, it will' is grounded in fact.

How big is the risk?

The next step is to try to assess the extent of the damage which may be done in the event of any of these possible risk scenarios developing fully. Again a 'worst case' analysis needs to be made since what one is trying to assess is the total degree of exposure.

Be realistic

Of course, one has to be realistic in this assessment and try not to overstate risk. It's very easy to let one's imagination run away during this kind of exercise and, although it may be great fun at the time, gross overstatement of highly improbable risks has the eventual effect of moving the whole operation beyond the realms of reality.

USING THE CHECK RISK PROGRAMME

This whole procedure is an extremely important one and it has two main purposes. Firstly, it provides a key piece of information in trying to work out just how extensive a reputation risk management programme is justified and, therefore, how much money and time should be devoted to it. Secondly, it provides the starting point for constructing the programme itself. By defining risk areas towards which attention should be given and by giving these areas a degree of weighting based on a combination of likelihood and potential severity, you actually pinpoint the priorities for action.

In addition, the very act of carrying through this exercise of risk assessment frequently has an even more basic result. It moves the entire notion of reputation risk management out of the world of general theory and focuses attention on what the absence of such activity might mean to your own business.

It is important during the exercise of setting up and running the risk check programme to remember that: **No list of risk areas will ever be complete. The unexpected is a part and parcel of reputation risk management**. However, the technique of starting with broad risk areas and narrowing these down to as many sub-areas of risk as possible means that a great deal of preparatory work will have been done. It will leave the reputation risk manager free to concentrate on specific aspects of problems as they are identified.

UPDATE

The technique also ensures that there is a clear identification of areas to watch and monitor in order to ensure that problems can be identified and dealt with, whenever possible, at an early stage. To reiterate a point made earlier, situations change and with the changing climate, the risks which may threaten an organisation may also mutate. Any check list programme must therefore have built into its structure regular reviews of its very fundamentals.

WORST POSSIBLE SCENARIOS

Unless you make this calculated assessment and, as far as possible, a specific listing of the sort of risks to reputation which threaten your business, one of two things happen. Either you do nothing and hope for the best in the belief that if the worst happens you can switch into crisis mode instantly and effectively. Alternatively, you put in place a generalised and non-focused programme, probably limited to crisis management, and believe that you are adequately covered.

It is difficult to be dogmatic about which is the worse of these two options. At least if you have done nothing when the crisis hits you know that you have to start from scratch. You will not be burdened by the false sense of security and false starts which result from a half worked through, generalised programme. On the other hand, even a general programme may be enough to prevent some of the more clumsy handling of crises which one sees in situations where management action has had the effect of making the bad much worse.

SUMMARY

In the absence of this fundamental procedure of risk assessment it is extremely likely that any reputation risk management programme which has been installed will be irrelevant in a number of areas and that key elements will not have been attended to. It also greatly increases the possibility of the completely avoidable crisis being allowed to develop, unmanaged and unseen. It's bad enough to try to manage a crisis unprepared and inadequately supported. It's worse to realise that much of the time a properly run reputation risk management programme would have ensured that there never was a crisis to manage in the first place.

Being in the midst of a crisis can be both stimulating and frightening and requires quite different skills from fulfilling a day-to-day management function. Without adequately laid down procedures, it can be rather like being adrift in a storm without a rudder. Without prepared physical support systems, it's like having a hole in the boat as well. Without some prior consideration of reputation risks and what they might entail, it's as if you've never been afloat before.

Summary points

- To be effective, the risk check programme must be:
  - comprehensive;
  - courageous, confronting 'worst possible' scenarios;
  - realistic;
  - tailored to each organisation/brand;
  - regularly reviewed.
- The programme can never be complete.
- The check sets priorities for action.

4 THE BOTTOM LINE OF RRM

A decision to institute and run a reputation risk management programme is a decision to invest. The investment will normally mean the allocation of time from management and other staff plus probably the direct cost of some involvement from outside consultants.

As with any form of investment, a clear decision needs to be taken at the outset about the level of commitment which is justified, or indeed whether the levels of risk faced justify any investment at all. For organisations where there is no previous formal commitment to reputation risk management, this may mean negotiating for budget with senior line management, possibly up to Board level. It is argued, in Chapter 6, that commitment to the principles of reputation risk management from the top of an organisation is essential for the success of any programme. The purpose of this chapter is to set out in some detail how the budget parameters of the programme should be structured, and how this expenditure equates to investment in an organisation's continuing success.

PRESENTING THE CASE

Since reputation risk management is concerned with prevention or, *in extremis*, with damage limitation there will never be a tangible return on the investment. The benefits obtained will never be fully quantifiable because one will only ever be able to guess at the consequences of not having such a programme. (One is reminded of the story of the PR man employed by a very shy tycoon with a morbid fear of kidnapping. Each year the PR man's formal presentation of his achievements was to produce a series of blank sheets of paper and to intone the words 'I kept you out of the Daily Mirror, I kept you out of the Star, I kept you out of the Herald Tribune, I kept you out of Newsweek . . .'.)

The decision of what level of investment to make, therefore, is undeniably partly a matter of judgement, both at individual and corporate level. However, the aspects of risk assessment which we have already looked at can be used to ensure that this judgement is an informed one and is not taken in a vacuum. If reputation risk management is to be taken seriously, the monies invested in it must be calculated within an agreed structure and not on the basis of 'What can we spare this year from promotions?' or even 'What should we have spent last year to avert the recall?'

Whilst return on this investment can never be quantifiable, it is equally important that, along with the budget, criteria for measuring effectiveness are agreed. No commercially competent organisation will commit itself indefinitely to a programme where there are no performance objectives.

Parallels with other risk management functions

When considering reputation risk management as an investment, it can be helpful to look at reputation risk management as being closely paralleled by the simple risk management function of a company as applied to credit control. Although the functions are not completely analogous there is a considerable degree of overlap.

Risk management of credit involves maintaining a continuous watch on the level of asset risk, acting to limit that risk as and when necessary and acting to limit damage in the event of disaster, often through credit insurance or part factoring of debts. In a similar way, reputation risk management involves the continuous monitoring of risk areas coupled with action to limit and head off potential problems at an early stage. It includes a programme to handle disasters, in the form of crisis management capability.

How much money and effort is put behind financial risk management is clearly determined by how great a risk is perceived. In a cash only business credit risk would be non-existent. For a business such as an advertising agency, which lays out money on its customers' behalf in anticipation of subsequent payment, credit risk can be potentially destructive of the business. It is hardly surprising that advertising agencies are heavy buyers of credit insurance and petrol stations are not.

The degree of exposure which is managed by the credit controller/ credit risk manager is the total book asset represented by debtors. For the reputation risk manager, the degree of exposure is the value of the business less its net physical assets and non-reputation related assets – for example, knowhow. As we have seen (Chapter 1), for all practical purposes this is determined by the price for a business (less these assets) which would be paid by a willing buyer in free market conditions. It is therefore the case that the value of assets which are at reputation risk are likely to be considerably greater than those at credit control risk – though degree of risk may be lower. This degree of risk is the second major factor which needs to be taken into account when considering the investment to be made in reputation risk management.

The exercise of identifying risks to reputation within specific areas, estimating the potential for damage of such risks on a 'worst case' scenario, and estimating the degree of likelihood against each of them, as discussed in Chapter 4, provides a basis for making a judgement about the total level of risk faced.

The parallels between credit control and reputation risk management diverge at this point. The credit controller seeks to minimise the total exposure to financial risk. Whereas, the reputation risk manager will see growth in exposure to reputation risk as an inexorable result of corporate or brand success. Both, however, have a prime responsibility to minimise the level of risk which relates to this exposure and to limit damage should such risk escalate into loss.

IS THE PRICE RIGHT?

Once these two assessments have been made – What is the value of assets at risk? What is the extent of that risk? – then there is at least a basis for saying 'This is the figure which we will invest in protecting our reputation'. In making this assessment it is clear that asset value is going to be high. The risk value is also going to be high – often to the point of near statistical certainty – that some risks will develop into problems and that, unmanaged, such problems will be damaging.

On any reasonable measure against other forms of protective activity and insurance the figure which is arrived at for a high asset value and a high level of risk will also be high – unacceptably high in commercial terms.

This is no reason for panic, it is almost certain that a great part of this investment is already being made.

What is already there?

In almost any organisation parts of the activity which have so far been subsumed into the general category of protecting against reputation risk will already be in place. For example:

- **Quality control** – The entire apparatus of quality control is, at least in part, geared towards the protection of the reputation of a company's products or services.

- **PR** – Where a company has a public relations programme it is likely that at least some part of this activity will be geared towards reputation protection, though often in an *ad hoc* and unstructured way.

- **Investor relations** – Some aspects of investor relations work will have a reputation protection element.

- **Market research** – The simple business of garnering market information and keeping abreast of industry developments means that a form of monitoring is already taking place.

- **Industrial relations** – If industrial relations has been identified as a potential reputation risk area, and it might well be, then there is likely to be some form of industrial relations activity in place beyond simple bargaining procedures.

In practice, therefore, proposed expenditure on reputation protection which is based only on considerations of asset value and perceived level of risk will be too high. We can subtract the cost of all of those elements of reputation risk management which are already in place under other guises.

SETTING THE BUDGET

The final calculation will look something like the following (figures used being totally arbitrary):

Table 4.1

Value of reputation asset		£1,000,000	
Level of risk justifies cost of protection plus insurance @		6.5%	
Therefore reputation risk management justified @		£65,000 per annum	
Existing investment p.a.		*% treated as RRM support*	*existing potential investment in RRM*
QC	£60,000	50%	£30,000
PR, investor relations	£40,000	25%	£10,000
Industry monitoring	£30,000	20%	£6,000
Total existing potential investment in RRM			£46,000
Justified additional expenditure on RRM		£19,000 per annum	

The 6.5% is a conservative percentage based on known levels for protection against fire risk and similar figures for the cost of debt protection.

This sample calculation highlights areas of inexactitude and assumptions. It serves to show, however, the basic principle for this way of approaching reputation risk management budgeting. In the real world, it is unlikely that a calculation such as this would be allowed to stand as a firm management guide to budgeting for a risk management programme. Quite apart from it containing too many assumptions for mathematical respectability, it simply is not the way that things happen in business. The exercise is, however, a necessary one. Not only does it provide a financial discipline within which to work, it also removes the discussion of investment in reputation protection from the sphere of the totally subjective and into the world of the logical, albeit with somewhat crude analytical techniques.

RE-EVALUATING EXISTING INVESTMENT

Carrying through the calculation has an additional benefit. It helps identify those activities already in place whose benefits are not being fully realised – indeed, some of which may be at least partly going to waste – because they are not contributing to an overall reputation risk management programme. In this context we are talking about liaison and co-operation and not the inappropriate taking over of functions within an organisation. Clearly, it is not true that everything which may be regarded as partially concerned with reputation protection should be placed under the control of the reputation risk management programme.

In the example given, Quality Control quite obviously should not come under any sort of reputation risk management control, despite being critical to the continued health of the reputation of the products or services. However, the investment in PR and allied activities, and the investment in information gathering and monitoring contain elements which can potentially make a real contribution with minimum extra cost or effort.

SUMMARY

The argument is, perhaps, in danger of becoming excessively theoretical but the conclusions are distinctly practical:

• A reputation risk management programme needs to establish and manage systems to identify and deal with potential crises before they have developed. In doing this it should draw on resources which already exist within a business and tap into information which is already being gathered or disseminated for other purposes.

- By looking at the value of assets at risk and the type and severity of the risk faced it is possible to assess (and sometimes as importantly justify) the level of investment to be made in such an activity.
- By identifying and weighting risk areas and looking at what is already done it is possible to identify what additional activities need to be put in place on a continuing basis and what activities need to be brought under reputation risk management controls.
- By identifying and weighting risk areas it is possible to fine-tune the standing crisis management programme which must be seen as a key part of any reputation risk management programme.

When it comes to the bottom line of reputation risk management, the question is not 'Can we afford to?' but, rather, 'Can we afford not to?'

Summary points

- Appropriate investment levels in RRM can be formally calculated.
- Don't panic – a percentage of this investment is already in place.

5 HOW IMPORTANT IS IT?

The arguments of the preceding chapters have been directed at affirming that reputation risk management is an important aspect of management. But is this really true? Are we not just making a huge song and dance about a few common sense precautions and activities which everyone takes into account anyway? Are we, perhaps, looking at yet another pompous statement of the obvious, combined with a few fancy labels, designed to inflate management importance and generate money for consultants?

The answer is no, we are not. The fact is that a great number of businesses do not take common sense precautions, nor do they undertake such routine activities. And, even if they do, these are usually quite inadequate to prevent, avert or deal with a situation where risk develops into threat and threat develops into crisis, let alone manage the sudden unavoidable crisis.

WHAT CAN HAPPEN – WHAT DID HAPPEN?

By their very nature reputation risk management and crisis management activities tend to be kept confidential and executives in the field are naturally reluctant to discuss particular case histories. There are, however, enough examples in the public domain to illustrate how ineptly otherwise highly intelligent and competent executives can act in mishandling or ignoring a risk to reputation.

To quote just four examples (two quite dramatic and two much smaller scale):

The problem of contamination of Perrier Water in 1989 was undoubtedly a blow to the company but the totally conflicting reactions and inconsistent positioning of the company by top executives throughout the world massively increased the impact during the first few days.

The Exxon oil spill in Alaska was an ecological disaster by any standards, but the company's apparent insensitivity and lack of anything other than commercial concern added a reputation element to the problems faced which may continue to have commercial consequences well into the future. (In contrast Occidental's obvious concern in handling the Piper Alpha Rig disaster had a major effect in limiting the damage to the company's reputation in the immediate aftermath.)

Towards the end of 1990, Gerald Ratner, head of the Ratner's Jewellers chain, grabbed headlines throughout the UK by claiming to make profits by 'selling crap' in a speech to the Institute of Directors. Although the company reacted well to adverse reaction in the popular press and attempted to counter punch at the point of sale, Ratner's gaffe came at a time of deep recession in retailing and with the peak Christmas sales period looming on the horizon. The consequences were predictable.

Following the Listeria in soft cheeses scare in Britain in 1988, the French cheese producers mounted a deliberately low key but highly directed campaign to get soft cheeses from France back on sale in retail outlets. While the health worry was successfully put into proportion, there remained a need to reassure the trade's commercial worries. At just this point the commercial sector of the French Embassy in London chose to give a prominent interview to 'The Grocer' (the key trade journal) attacking the British Government and underlining the commercial disaster to French cheese which had occurred. Once again the reactions of the buyers for the big supermarket chains were predictable.

The list could go on and on and would still only represent the tip of an iceberg. In each of these cases it is clear that lack of a reputation risk management discipline exacerbated or, in the Ratner example, actually created the problem faced. In each case we are considering extremely successful and, in general, highly professional organisations. The fact that a failure to anticipate, prevent, deflect or manage reputation threatening situations occurs in otherwise well-managed organisations is important. It is the clearest possible indication that **reputation risk management is not simply a matter of common sense or simply a formal way of describing generally applied techniques**.

If no formal structure exists then things are missed, mistakes are made, there is no clear point of responsibility and panic can ensue. Without adequate information and without back-up systems management operates at worst in total ignorance and at best with one hand tied behind its back. We are, after all, considering systems to protect an asset of great value and not some minor aspect of business operation. It is not sufficient protection for such an asset to hope for the best and try to cobble together some sort of reaction when it appears that a risk has developed into a genuine threat.

We know that risk is an ever present factor in the business environment and we know that the risks which apply to reputation are just as real as any other – just as reputation is an asset as real as any other. Although it has been argued that reputation has had value since the very start of trade – Og and his well thought of flint arrowheads – and that this reputation has always been at risk – rumours of Og's failing sight around the caves – the fact is that **the levels of risk and the value of reputations have grown enormously in recent years**. The consequent importance of reputation risk management has grown in parallel.

GLOBAL WARNING

There are two major factors which have contributed to this situation – the growth of international business and the growth of global communications. Each of these developments may be seen as being dependent on, and feeding off, the other, with one notable, marketing consequence being the development of global brands.

It is clear that as companies create and develop global brands, these brands are likely to be of considerably greater value than individual brands developed for a specific market place. There have been progressive moves by companies to internationalise their brands both by seeking world markets for nationally developed products and by standardising naming, present-ation and positioning of products which already enjoy worldwide sales. (A good example of a company doing both of these things is the US confectionery giant Mars, world leader in confectionery sales and generally regarded as being one of the most astute marketing companies around. During the '80s Mars successfully 'globalised' its 'M&M's' brand by inter-nationalising its production and marketing. At the same time, Mars stan-dardised products which had been sold under different names in different markets – for example 'Snickers' which had been sold as 'Marathon' in the strong UK confectionery market.)

Global brands have global values and they also face global risks. We have discussed previously the case of 'Tylenol' and the effects on the brand of consumer terrorism. As it happens 'Tylenol' was, and is, a huge brand but not a global one. Had it been, there can be no question that the crisis which Johnson and Johnson faced over the brand would have been on a global rather than a North American scale.

What is true of brands is also true in a different way of companies themselves. There are more truly international companies today than there have ever been and there are more companies which, even though nationally based, rely on an international market place to sell their products and services.

As with global brands, this may mean that such companies have a bigger investment in their corporate reputations as a result of internationalisation, although this does not necessarily follow. What does follow is that the potential risk to reputation is spread wider geographically and, given the quality and extent of today's communications network, when something goes wrong anywhere a company operates then it will rapidly be known everywhere that company operates. It is far, far harder today to confine the effects of a crisis on a company's reputation geographically than it has ever been. In the interests of public information this is, perhaps, a very good thing. But it can mean that a false rumour started in, say, Tokyo can see people refusing to buy product in New York within hours. Thus internationalisation and increased scope of communications have contributed to increased value of reputation and increased levels of risk. There are also other factors.

REPUTATIONS GET BIGGER

There has been an increasing awareness of the value of reputation in recent years and a consequent increase of investment in building reputation which, in turn, has resulted in a further increase in the value of that intangible asset. (One indication of this is the mushroom growth of the PR industry nationally and on a global scale – an industry which barely existed prior to the Second World War.) There has been a progressive move away from generic products and towards branded goods, creating new and more brand values. The efforts and investment by major supermarket chains and other retailers in building up reputation for their 'own label' is a significant pointer in this context.

The increasingly competitive market environment has made the launching of new products into an established sector progressively harder and, consequently, increased the value of existing brands with an established reputation and market share. All of these developments have operated to increase the value of reputation – or more accurately, the value of the assets which are vulnerable to damage or loss of reputation.

RISKS MOUNT

Risk areas for reputation have increased as well.

The very fact that business has grown progressively more complicated makes it that much easier to create totally unnecessary crises through crossed wires within an organisation. (We will look more closely at this danger later.)

The sheer volume of information and opinion bombarding today's public makes the possibility of often unfounded criticism more likely. There is far greater public concern about products, services and companies than there has been in the past. This means one must be prepared not only to take the correct action, but to explain and convince as well.

The growth of consumer terrorism and extortion only threatens part of the business community but that part is a very big one.

Increased complexity and quantity of Government legislation and Government comment have the potential for often unintentional disastrous consequences for particular businesses.

The above list is not comprehensive but serves to show how reputation risk is increasing, and there are no significant areas where risk has diminished.

WHO DOES NOT NEED RRM?

These factors do not all apply to all organisations, and some apply to none. Not every organisation needs to install a reputation risk management programme any more than every organisation needs to install a main frame computer. The requirement is partly a function of size, partly a function of risk exposure and partly a matter of judgement as to how much benefit such a programme could be to a particular organisation in protecting against risk. There are instances of companies with a high investment in reputation and a high exposure to reputation risk which, none the less, would gain only minimal potential benefit from the type of programme under discussion here.

Typically, companies producing a limited range of high capital value products for a very limited customer base, perhaps in the defence industry, would wish to create a reputation protection programme which bears little resemblance to the type of catch-all programme required by the open market place.

AND WHO DOES?

Formal risk management programmes are of most value to medium- to large-sized companies operating in the open market and to smaller companies with a high investment in reputation and a high perceived level of reputation risk.

Simply because reputation is an intangible asset and because there are such a variety of ways in which reputation may be put at risk, it is more difficult to set out a clear programme for managing reputation risk than it is for other disciplines which may be associated with managing a crisis or with protecting against risk exposure.

The procedures for product recall, for example, are complex. But, in terms of the mechanics of the operation, they can be set out quite clearly as a decision tree and programme of activities. Rules for operating a credit control system are, similarly, capable of being set down in an unambiguous way and may, for the greater part, be implemented at a fairly junior executive level.

Reputation risk management tends to require the exercise of judgement at almost every stage of its operation which results in some blurring of the simple rules. It also operates as an integrated part of a business with overlapping concerns and responsibilities and a consequential difficulty in determining just where it should start and end.

The very fact that there are these, admitted, areas of difficulty makes it that much more imperative that there should be a clear allocation of responsibility, that rules and guidelines should be firmly established, and that procedures should be clearly understood. Reputation risk management does require a process of continuous decision making. Decisions made in a vacuum, with insufficient information or without a framework of rules and guidelines are likely to be wrong decisions. In fact, formalising reputation risk protection into a managed programme is precisely the opposite of creating mystique and work for management and consultants. It is a process of demystifying an aspect of business which is all too often characterised by much talk and little action, muddled attitudes and ineffective procedures.

Summary points

- Reputation risk management is not 'just common sense'.
- Reputation risk factors are growing incrementally.
- Not every organisation needs a reputation risk management programme.

'AT THE COALFACE'
Goalkeepers not just goalstoppers

Crisis Management grabs the headlines when it successfully handles 'the big one'. In the Parliamentary arena this may mean questions on the floor of the House, Ministerial promises to look again at proposed legislation, headlines and debate in the press and eventual modification of some measure which would have severely damaged an industry sector or company. Such high profile activity usually results in considerable relief from the party at risk and, in the tight world of the Parliamentary lobbyist, applause and respect for the consultant who marshalled the arguments and the contacts to rescue the threatened party from the jaws of disaster.

It's like the goalkeeper in a Cup Final who, with lightning reactions, tips the ball round the post to prevent an apparently certain equaliser in the dying seconds of the game. Good goalkeepers make great saves quite often. Great goalkeepers organise the defence, read the game, see potential trouble early and act as goalkeepers rather than goal stoppers – of course they also make great saves when they have to.

Good crisis management is something like good goalkeeping. It may be the great saves which get talked about in the pub after the game but it is the ability to read the game early which counts overall.

Lord Irving of Dartford, now sadly deceased, acted as a Parliamentary Consultant for a number of clients and worked primarily with the PR Consultancy Gwynne Hart and Associates. Sidney Irving was a long serving Labour MP representing Dartford and became Deputy Speaker of the House of Commons before accepting a Life Peerage and moving to the House of Lords. His knowledge of Parliamentary procedures and of people was encyclopaedic, his record as a constituency MP exemplary and his popularity high.

In 1979/80 he spotted a piece of proposed legislation going through the committee stages of the House of Commons by which all meat which had been judged 'unfit for human consumption' would have to be dyed bright green. The intention of this was quite obviously to prevent the illegal resale of unfit meat to the consumer. Apart from any problems which might arise in the practical implementation of this proposed measure by the slaughter houses this was hardly a proposal which would seem to have an impact on anyone trading legitimately in fast-moving consumer goods. Certainly not something to set the alarm bells ringing in a major sector of the grocery industry and one which had established the highest standards of care and quality control – with a record of strict compliance with regulations and a deal of voluntary controls and standards.

The prepared petfood industry is huge in Europe and the United States, and the UK is the single strongest market. Annual sales of canned prepared petfoods for cats and dogs in the UK were valued at £850 million (US$1.5 billion) in 1990. The best selling canned cat food is the single largest grocery brand in the United Kingdom. People buy prepared petfood because they know that it provides a well balanced diet for their pet and because their pet likes it. In general people are perfectly well aware that food fit for animal consumption is not necessarily passed fit for human consumption. But imagine the average pet owner's reaction on opening a can of meaty dog or cat food and finding the contents bright green! Indeed, many pet owners do not even wish to be reminded that the canned food that they feed to their pet has not been passed fit for them to eat themselves.

Lord Irving was perfectly well aware of this. One of Gwynne Hart's clients was the largest producer of prepared petfood in the UK.

With no fuss or public outcry the proposed legislation was killed at the Committee Stages.

This was not achieved through any special dealing but rather through detailed and thought out submissions to the relevant committee setting out just what the consequences of such a bill would be to the prepared petfood industry and, indirectly, to pets and their owners. The long term professionalism of the Pet Food Manufacturers Association and the industry's record of open and ethical dealing made it certain that the arguments put forward would be given due weight. A standing programme of keeping MPs informed about this major industry and related areas, such as responsible pet ownership, ensured that members of the committee were already aware of the context and background to the arguments. Submissions to the committee were made by the petfood manufacturers. Lord Irving's role, and that of the Gwynne Hart management team, was that of co-ordinators and advisers.

Lord Irving and his colleagues at Gwynne Hart, notably Norman Hart spotted the danger early, marshalled the defence and deflected potential trouble without damage to business or to reputation. They achieved this because the danger was spotted early, because a great deal of groundwork had already been done and because a lot of hard, professional work was put in to presenting the case in the right form.

No doubt the proposed legislation could have been changed on the floor of the House of Commons or at a very late stage in the committee procedures. No doubt such a change and the debate which preceded it would have been widely reported (Britain is, indeed, a nation of pet lovers). No doubt a large number of pet owners would have been quite needlessly upset and the prepared petfood industry would have suffered some damage. No doubt a successful outcome for the industry achieved at a late stage in the proceedings would have been hailed as a triumph of crisis management.

Sidney Irving himself would probably have seen the whole issue as hard work but routine. In any event he undoubtedly regarded his Parliamentary Consultancy work as being quite unimportant compared with his role as a Parliamentarian. To the observer, however, it seems a perfect example of reputation risk management carried through to total success through well applied systems and an element of flair.

I have no idea whether Lord Irving ever played football but I know he would have made a great goalkeeper.

6 WHOSE RESPONSIBILITY IS IT?

It is all very well agreeing that there should be a programme of activity designed to protect reputation and that this programme should be applied to any and all aspects of an organisation's activity where reputation assets are involved. Somebody, or somebodies, have to take responsibility for such a programme, ensure that it keeps running on a steady basis (although at times this involves very little obviously proactive work), make sure that it is adequately budgeted, regularly reviewed and generally follows specialist management functions and disciplines.

THE RRM MANAGER

Whilst overall responsibility for the programme may be handled by a team of people from within an organisation, drawing on specialist skills, it is essential that an individual is appointed to manage the programme. This in itself will help to clarify areas of ambiguity and overlap which constantly threaten to muddy the waters of reputation risk management. Whilst it must be carried out in consultation, reputation risk management must never be by consensus. The correct decisions cannot be made by default.

The very nature of reputation risk management, for the vast majority of the time, is concerned with identifying and tracking risk and with taking appropriate action to deflect such risk. In order to do this effectively, the manager of the programme must be in a position to know what such risks are, irrespective of what areas of a business' activities are involved. Moreover he or she must have the authority to enforce tracking procedures and early warning systems in departments which do not fall under his or her direct control. For that relatively small portion of the time when reputation risk management turns into crisis management, the reputation risk manager must have the authority and knowledge to act as a full member of the crisis team.

(It may well not be the case that a designated 'crisis manager' is the same person who runs the reputation risk management programme, indeed it is unlikely. But a reputation risk manager has to be at the very core of the team and cannot be handicapped by huge gaps in company status).

IS IT A PR FUNCTION?

Reputation is, frequently, an asset which may be seen to rest somewhere between the marketing and external, corporate or public relations functions of an organisation. The skills and techniques required for effective reputation risk management are mainly to be found in these areas too, with an emphasis on the public relations function.

It would seem fairly obvious, then, that the responsibility for reputation risk management should rest within an organisation's public relations department, assuming that it has one, or with whoever has responsibility for public relations activity. Obvious it may be, but in practice this may very well be a mistaken view to take.

Levels of seniority

In large organisations, the corporate relations director, or executive of similar title, may have a high level of seniority. He or she is unlikely to sit on the Board proper but may well have something very close to Board status. In the case of smaller organisations, the PR function is unlikely to be given this sort of weight and the 'in house' responsibility for PR will be in the hands of a publicity manager. It is in no way to disparage the skills of the 'in house' PR person to say that without the access to information and the overall perspective on a business' operations, normally only obtainable at Board level, it is an impossible task to take overall responsibility for a reputation risk management programme.

The outside consultant

Where a business employs outside PR consultants there may be an argument for using the consultancy to manage the programme, answerable to a suitably senior executive of the company – ideally the chief executive. Consultants have the advantage of not being trapped within a company's line management structure and moreover will be more likely to take an objective view of things.

In this situation the problem is likely to be lack of information. An outside consultant will only know as much as he or she is told and, although most professional PR firms will demand and get access to Board level executives as needed, access is a very long way from regular, in depth briefing.

Shift in PR emphasis

There is another problem in making reputation risk management a purely PR responsibility, and this probably applies more strongly to 'in house' executives, however senior, than it does to the outside consultant. If reputation risk management is seen as an exclusive concern of the PR function of an organisation this tends to mean that it becomes subsumed in the routine PR operations of that organisation. It is not clearly recognised as a discipline in its own right. Therefore it is not given as much senior attention as other forms of risk management and is, as a consequence, under budgeted.

Despite the Institute of Public Relations definition of PR as 'The deliberate and planned effort to establish and maintain mutual understanding between an organisation and its publics', the practical application of PR is far more often to be defined along the lines of 'The deliberate and planned effort to project positive messages about a organisation and its products and services to its publics'. This shift in emphasis from 'mutual understanding' to 'projecting positive messages' is a perfectly legitimate utilisation of PR techniques but it does mean that a PR function focused in this direction will not be orientated towards management of reputation risk. This emphasis on 'positive message' PR is implicitly recognised in a great number of businesses where the PR function is run by the publicity manager who is answerable to the marketing or, sometimes, sales director.

The corporate relations director

Where a company has a corporate relations director then this is very likely to be the best person to take responsibility for the reputation risk management programme. The very fact that an appointment at this level of seniority has been made in the area of corporate relations usually means that the company already takes reputation seriously and that the corporate relations director, even if not a *bone fide* full Board member, will have the proper level of access to information and sufficient authority to ensure that the programme runs properly both in routine and in crisis mode. (This may not always be the case – there are many fine titles masking fairly routine jobs – but as a general rule it will be a reasonable yardstick.)

ACTIONING THE RRM PROGRAMME

Running a reputation risk management programme must, then, be a Board level or equivalent responsibility. Clearly most of the activity undertaken will be delegated either to the PR function or to outside consultants, or to both, but there will need to be a continuous input from the top. This input will need to include:

- active participation in risk identification and assessment;
- routine checks to ensure that everyone is doing their jobs;
- a degree of decision-making on a running basis;
- in crisis mode, total commitment.

The job of being responsible for reputation risk management is, in short, an active responsibility and one which can only be carried through effectively at a senior level.

The consultants

In practice, determining strategy and budgets will not be a one man decision but should be worked through at Board level. The active input of information on an organisation's other risk management commitments from staff with specialist line responsibilities is strongly recommended at this stage. The precise make up of the senior group involved in strategy, budgeting and updating of a reputation risk management programme will depend on the internal structure of the business involved. But there must at least be provision for regular financial, marketing and corporate inputs.

The use of outside consultants to contribute to the programme is also usually extremely useful. Because of their experience of handling such programmes across a range of clients, consultants can bring a perspective and a level of hands on experience to bear which is rarely available 'in house'. The advantages of objectivity and freedom from line management restriction have already been mentioned. Just how big a role should be given to consultants will depend entirely on circumstances. But the practice which has developed of calling them in to help out only after a crisis has developed is clearly not the best way to make use of their skills.

Administration

Provided the programme is properly worked out and responsibility is placed at the right level of seniority, there are a host of different ways in which reputation risk management can be handled administratively. The most effective method will depend very much on the structure and culture of the business concerned. For any particular business, however, there will be a number of restrictions and the preferred administrative method will be best arrived at by 'jobbing back' from the programme itself.

All reputation risk management programmes share a number of rules, procedures, techniques and physical requirements in common. The terminology employed may vary. Lines of responsibility will depend on individual company structures. The level of importance given to the programme may differ from company to company, but the main elements of a professionally run programme remain very much the same.

REVIEW – CHAPTERS 1–6

We have now reached the point at which we can look at reputation risk management programmes themselves and set out the practical elements which go to make up such a programme.

Before doing so, however, it is probably sensible to pause for a second and review what has been argued during the first six chapters. While not particularly controversial, the points which are made and the method of looking at reputation risk are, as yet, far from being universally adopted. A point by point summary may be of help in separating the bare bones of the argument from the surrounding commentary.

1 Reputation has value and this value is practically demonstrated every time a 'goodwill' element is included in a sales price, in the prices paid for brands, in balance sheet values of brands and in stock valuations of companies above physical assets.

2 Good company practice demands protection/insurance of company assets. Reputation is such an asset.

3 Reputation is a peculiarly vulnerable asset, being threatened by random risks. It is directly a function of perception, not necessarily reality.

4 Reputation is a necessary, if not sufficient, part of brand value and of other intangible assets. Therefore the 'insurance' value of the reputation of such assets equals their value (price to a willing buyer in a free market).

5 A rough calculation of the reasonable level of spend on protecting reputation can be arrived at by considering:
   - value of asset to be protected;
   - level and extent of risk involved;
   - existing expenditure devoted to, or potentially devoted to, reputation protection.

6 Reputation risk management requires a continuing commitment and is at least as concerned with prevention and early warning systems as with 'crisis management'.

7 The requirement for formal systems to provide a reputation protection programme is a growing one. Both the value of individual reputation assets and the level and extent of risk faced continue to increase.

8 The responsibility for running a reputation risk management programme must be placed at a senior level and cannot be absorbed into the day-to-day PR operations of a company. The manager of the programme must have:
   - access to a full range of company information;
   - a business wide perspective on reputation and risk;
   - authority to enforce decisions routinely and in crisis.

7 THE BONES OF AN RRM PROGRAMME AND RISK ASSESSMENT REVISITED

Reputation risk management (from this point onwards we will adopt the acronym *RRM* since the phrase 'reputation risk management should, by now, have become sufficiently familiar) is a continuing process and needs to operate as such. It is a mistake to regard work in this area as being something which can be turned on and off like a tap or to feel that there is only a need for such activity to be implemented when a major crisis threatens.

In some respects, such a programme will be like paying insurance premiums in that it involves outlay which it is hoped will never lead to a claim. Although any realistic analysis will show that a business of any substance is almost statistically certain to face the unavoided crisis on occasion, but this will only be one aspect of the programme. In other respects the programme will show a continuing and direct benefit by making sure that exposure to unnecessary risk is avoided, that manageable areas of reputation risk are prevented from developing into threats and that these potential crises headed off before they have developed.

The different parts of the programme may be regarded as distinct from each other but, in practice, they will overlap. Moreover the efficient operation of any one part of the programme will depend on other elements of the programme being in place and being operated with a similar efficiency. For example:

- Contacts and lines of communication established to deal with potential crises before they have developed will continue to be of value in a full blown crisis scenario.
- The process of monitoring for potential risk areas will be of value both in avoiding unnecessary risk and in providing early warning for developing problems.
- The initial exercise of identifying risk areas will be directly relevant to all sections of the programme.
- The very process of setting up procedures for risk avoidance and for risk

control is invaluable pre-training for crisis handling.

- Clearance loops and internal information systems which need to be established are common to all aspects of RRM.
- Perhaps most important of all, the day-to-day management of an RRM creates an attitude and approach, even a business culture, which can deal with potential and actual crises in a calm and considered manner. If there is one single quality which is called for in RRM, it is the ability to keep cool.

The bones of an RRM programme are fairly straightforward and have been anticipated in the preceding chapters of this book. They are interlinked, and any attempt to implement a part of such a programme in isolation is likely to severely limit its effectiveness. It is important to recognise this from the start and to set up the full programme taking into account all the various functions which it will be expected to fulfil. Failure to do this makes subsequent modification of the programme very difficult, particularly where the part of the programme which has been put in place in isolation is the crisis management element – a function which should be a development of a full programme and should grow out of the more routine systems already in place.

In the absence of underlying attention to anticipating, avoiding and deflecting risk, a purely crisis management programme is likely to be invoked more frequently than is necessary, to lose a great part of its edge, and eventually to corrode into something short of proper preparedness for the serious, unavoided crisis.

In the absence of a crisis management programme the activity carried out in risk anticipation and avoidance will still have value but it will lack the ultimate ability to cope with occasions when reputation is placed most severely at risk. Moreover, as we will see in discussion of the escalating crisis, it is often necessary to have full crisis handling capability in order to deal with the intermediate stages during which a crisis develops and to prevent it reaching major proportions, despite the fact that in such a situation it may never be necessary to go into full crisis management mode. Simply because the continuing operation of an RRM programme is not spectacular and management of crisis is, there is a tendency to ignore the need for the one until events plunge one into the midst of the other.

It sometimes takes experience of a major crisis to focus a company's attention on the need to be prepared to deal with any similar or parallel situation in the future. Assuming that there is still a company left to deal with the future, then the experience of having had to deal with a major incident is the most salutary lesson imaginable. It is at this point that the corporate relations director, the PR consultancy, or whoever, is likely to be required by the board to put formal plans in place for the future. And it is at this point that the opportunity should be taken to ensure that such plans involve a complete programme and not simply a set of rules to ensure that, if the same thing happens again, the company will be better prepared.

If this seems an overly cynical attitude towards senior management's attitude to planning for crisis then the findings of two recent surveys of such attitudes may be of interest.

The first was conducted in the USA by Lexicon Communications and found that of the chief executives of companies questioned, 89% believed a crisis in business 'as inevitable as death or taxes'. However only 50% of the sample questioned claimed to have a plan to deal with one, should it arise.

In the UK, Regester plc surveyed 80 of The Times top 1000 companies on their perceived vulnerability to some form of corporate crisis. Less than 30% of the sample believed themselves vulnerable to any form of corporate crisis and even fewer had undertaken any form of risk analysis or put in place any kind of procedures or training programmes to prepare themselves for damage limitation should such a crisis occur.*

From my own experience I can confirm that on every occasion that my company has been involved in installing an RRM or crisis management programme it has been as a result of a company actually facing such a crisis or having become aware of a need because of an incident which has occurred within their particular business sector. (All too often the call for help comes right in the middle of a disaster for which no pre-planning at all has been carried out and things are already going noticeably wrong.)

In the relatively calm atmosphere of normal business, plans for an RRM programme can be set down away from the pressures of a crisis in action or away from the inquest and recriminations on a crisis which has just been survived.

The bare bones of such a programme are not complicated:-

- **Risk assessment** – the logical starting point for any programme and a necessary first activity.
- **Risk avoidance** – managing risk and limiting damage is valuable but where risk can be eliminated completely this is obviously better still. This should be a part of the RRM programme even though it will frequently involve considerations which go beyond the normal parameters of such a programme (see Chapter 8).

---

* I am indebted to Michael Regester, Managing Director of Regester plc, for drawing my attention to these two surveys.

- **Risk anticipation** – There are a great number of risks to reputation which can be anticipated with a fair degree of accuracy and prepared for in advance. Sometimes a potential crisis simply cannot be anticipated, but many reputation risks develop from risk to threat and from threat to crisis. This allows opportunities to act while the threat is still developing. Early warning systems and early action to head off danger are always to be preferred to full blown crisis management, however efficient this may be.
- **Risk management** – As long as one is managing reputation risk one is in a position to dictate, or at least heavily influence, events. The day-to-day management of reputation risk will prevent the development of reputation crises and will also protect a business against those smaller attacks on reputation which may be damaging but which are not of crisis proportions.
- **Crisis preparation** – The worst time to learn about crisis management is while actually doing the job. Time spent making sure that there is a fully prepared crisis handling plan, that support systems are in place and that people are trained and practised is time infinitely well spent. Then one can only hope that they will never be called into action!
- **Crisis management** – No two crises are ever the same and however good the preparation there will always be decisions to take and judgements to be exercised.

Each of these elements in an RRM programme involves a variety of activities which deserve to be looked at in greater detail.

There has already been some discussion of risk assessment. Previous comments on the subject were in the context of deciding on the form and extent which an RRM programme should take. In some respects, this activity can be considered as a preliminary to the programme proper, but not entirely. It is worth briefly considering risk assessment as a part of the continuing RRM programme.

RISK ASSESSMENT AS A CONTINUING PROCESS

Risk changes as a company itself changes. This may be by introducing new products or practices, entering new markets, acquiring new subsidiaries or simply through the process of growth itself. It may also be through changes in the economic and social environment in which the company operates.

We are concerned with the management of risk to reputation and we have already seen that reputation is a direct function of perception. From this it follows that a change in the perspective from which perceptions are formed will have an effect on what constitutes a risk to reputation. A change in social, political or economic attitudes may mean the emergence of whole new areas of risk or, more likely, changes in the weighting and importance which should be given to identified risk areas.

Perhaps more obviously, specific events in the world beyond a business' commercial activities can have a direct impact on reputation risks connected with those activities. A fairly dramatic example of this would be the different ways in which trade between an American company and Iraq would be regarded through the eighties as Saddam Hussein's regime moved from being regarded as one more Middle Eastern country, to the 'bastion against the fundamentalist fanatics of Iran' and then on to 'international terrorists and pariah among nations'. At a more predictable level, changes of Government, changes in legislation, scientific discoveries or advances and the like can have impact on all aspects of a business' operations, including exposure to reputation risk.

Risk assessment should not, therefore, be a once and once only activity at the start of a programme but should be an exercise which is repeated formally at regular intervals. This formal review might well take place on an annual basis. If the exercise discussed previously, aimed at determining the proper level at which to allocate resources to RRM activity, is carried out annually then a formal reassessment of risk will be a logical part of such an exercise. If the budgeting exercise is not repeated in a formal way, then the process of risk assessment should still take place.

The need for this formal review does not preclude the continuing pattern of modification to perceived risk which will result from the operation of an RRM programme. Through continuous monitoring and through early warning systems there will be a constant shifting of attention to risk and a constant shifting of weighting given to particular risk areas. If there is not, then the systems are not working.

However, experience shows that this rolling process of risk assessment is carried out too close to the issues faced to allow the general perspective and objective stand point necessary for an overall assessment of the total area of risk. The classic situation of the urgent superseding the important on a day-to-day basis is not confined to risk assessment, but it certainly applies. A regular formal review restores perspective and reminds everyone of priorities. It helps ensure that in dealing with a number of mini-crises one does not overlook the major crisis when it appears.

The assessment of risk is at the foundation of any RRM programme. In looking at the other areas of the programme and at the specific activities which should be carried out, either in preparation or in action, there must be an underlying assumption that there is a continuous reference back to the findings of the risk assessment analysis. It is this analysis which defines those areas of perceived risk which the entire programme is designed to protect against.

8 ELIMINATING RISK

Prevention is always better than cure and this applies at every stage of RRM. The entire aim of a programme is damage limitation and there is no more effective way to do this than by eliminating risk in the first place. Of course, there is no way to do this entirely. Reputation risk is a near certain consequence of being in business, and it is no part of an RRM programme to recommend the closing down of a business.

Less extremely, there will often be business activity which exposes a company to reputation risk and which might be regarded as potentially disposable but where the commercial benefit is obviously substantial. Once again it is clear that giving excessive weight to considerations of reputation risk would be a case of the tail wagging the dog and it is no part of RRM to act against a company's fundamental commercial interests.*

There are three aspects of risk elimination which deserve consideration and which I have called – Tower of Babel, The Unbalanced Equation and Pre-emptive Strike.

TOWER OF BABEL

A careful look at an organisation's perceived exposure to reputation risk will frequently expose unnecessary areas of risk which can be eliminated without

---

* I should make it clear here that we are considering commercial and not moral issues. It is no part of the argument that an RRM manager should close his or her eyes to unethical business practice on the grounds that the profits outweigh the chances and consequences of being discovered. This is an ethical rather than an RRM question and applies to every member of an organisation aware of such a situation, irrespective of that person's area of responsibility. There are, however, certain circumstances in which RRM can act as a force for improved business ethics within an organisation – even if the basis of such influence is commercial rather than moral (see Chapter 24).

excessive changes to company policy or procedures. Let us consider a couple of fictional examples, both based fairly closely on real events.

A company exporting significant quantities of product to the Middle East discovers that it is in danger of being blacklisted in the area because of supposed manufacturing facilities in Israel. The company does sell product to Israel but does not manufacture or obtain materials from there. In these circumstances there are no formal grounds for the company to be placed on the blacklist but Damascus can be fairly idiosyncratic in decisions of this nature and very careful and delicate representations have to be made. At this point a quite separate part of the company announces a major contract to supply product to South Africa – having weighed the risk to reputation from those people who favour a boycott of that country and decided that the positive news of the overseas order outweighs this (the company being British and the year 1987). South Africa is the other country where manufacture or obtaining materials can lead to an Arab world boycott. Still the company has not contravened boycott rules by simply selling product. But the association with South Africa, on top of the association with Israel, is too much for the boycott office in Damascus. The company is blacklisted and the entire Middle East market is lost.

A company pursues a routine policy of analyst and financial journalist briefings as part of its City PR programme. These briefings are held over lunch and are attended by the chief executive and arranged by the company's PR consultancy. The board gets wind of a possible takeover bid for the company which it will certainly wish to contest, but information is far from certain. Not wishing to expose himself to City gossip prematurely, the chief executive tells the PR Consultancy to cancel two briefing sessions due to be held over the next two days, but does not inform the consultancy why. Since the briefings are routine no particular explanation is given by the consultancy although cancellation, particularly at such short notice, is totally out of character. Drawing their own erroneous conclusions, and with interim results due fairly soon, two of the journalists speculate on the company's performance and general financial health. When the hostile bid is announced some ten days later it is against a depressed share price and the first round of the takeover battle is lost before the first shot has been fired.

The incidental details given in these two examples are fictional but the essential scenarios really occurred. In both cases real risk was created by the companies concerned due to a failure of internal lines of communication. Failing to make sure that the right hand knows what the left hand is doing presents an area of unnecessary reputation risk and one which can be eliminated by the simple procedure of ensuring that any external statements of any significance, or any actions which impinge directly on reputation building activity, are checked through a central clearing house. This may sound excessively bureaucratic but, intelligently managed, it does not need to be. The 'policeman' role of clearance can always be tempered by commonsense.

The two examples given show how risk can be increased by a failure of internal communication. Risk can also be created out of nothing in the same way. Consider the effects on previously perfectly amicable industrial relations of the ill-timed, over-bullish comments of the board at a time of wage negotiation; or the endlessly amazing way in which senior politicians of the same party can say flatly contradictory things in public to different audiences creating an impression of muddle and confusion; or the failure to cancel high profile advertising campaigns when circumstances have made them inappropriate e.g. safety claims at a time of car recall for adjustment; or the comments made by Gerald Ratner to the Institute of Directors discussed previously (see Chapter 5)

Such failures to communicate generally result from a specialisation in the interests of those making the public statements. Gerald Ratner apart (and in all fairness, it is excessive to lay the blame for the chain's hiccup in performance entirely at the door of his comments, however ill-judged), the examples given are all cases of people acting perfectly properly within their own terms. The problems arise when those terms are too narrow and an overall perspective has not been taken. It is precisely this overall perspective which is needed in an RRM programme and it is precisely when overall perspective is present that this category of unnecessary risk can be eliminated at source.

THE UNBALANCED EQUATION

Failure to communicate is not the sole cause of avoidable risk. In general, elimination of other risk areas will involve a change in commercial activity and, consequently, the taking of decisions which have an impact which goes beyond RRM or internal information procedures. This does not mean that they should not be of any concern to the RRM manager but only that reputation risk considerations will be only one of a number of inputs to consideration of such potential risk areas.

Although it is true that RRM should not be allowed to dictate to corporate decisions, it is also the case that where a business is involved in activity which is of small commercial benefit, but which represents significant corporate reputation risk, then the right commercial decision will be to eliminate that risk by changing or ceasing that activity. This sort of situation can sometimes occur following an acquisition, when a company takes on board a whole series of businesses and business practices, none of which was the prime reason for the acquisition in the first place. It can also come about through growth when the activities of some outposts of the business empire become remote from central policy and relatively autonomous in activity. It can occur where an organisation's investment policy, or even its pension fund investment policy, has led to holdings in companies which are in direct conflict with the main thrust of the company's business and its overall corporate philosophy.

Examples of the type of case, where serious consideration needs to be given to the balance between commercial benefit and reputation risk, might be:

A company operating in an essentially 'dirty' industry has a good record for pollution control and has invested in promoting its reputation in this area. On acquiring another company in a similar business, it discovers that one or more of the bought company's sites, although operating perfectly legally, are close to allowed pollution guidelines and have faced a high level of local criticism.

A textile and fashion company, having expanded hugely, has a major market in natural and man-made fibre cloths and finished garments. It continues to operate a small, traditional furriers using wild and farmed animal skins as a marginally profitable operation dating from the early days of the company's history.

A company which has based its industrial relations policy on worker participation and open wage negotiations has built superb union relations and has a strike free record based on mutual trust. The company's investment arm has invested heavily in Third World mining operations with appalling work conditions and a record of 'slave labour'.

In two of these imaginary cases the perceived threat comes from ecological considerations. This emphasis is intentional. It has already been pointed out that the changing social climate in which one operates can mean that reputation risks emerge where none existed before, and in no area is this more noticeable at the moment than in that of increased environmental awareness.

Although these are imaginary, similar examples abound in the real world and in each case it might well be felt that reputation risk outweighs any commercial benefits which may accrue – the equation is unbalanced.

THE PRE-EMPTIVE STRIKE

It is not always necessary to change business practice to handle a perceived risk to reputation, nor is it always necessary to let a perceived risk stand and to put in procedures to manage it, should it develop towards becoming a threat. It may be possible to eliminate a perceived risk by making a pre-emptive strike.

This is, without doubt, a strategy which should be approached with caution. The last thing that one wants to do is to precipitate a crisis by focusing attention on a potential risk area in a way which results in a real problem blowing up. There is a natural wish to leave well alone when looking at possible risk areas and to reassure oneself with the thought that careful monitoring and a proper RRM programme will keep things firmly under control. However, this is not always the best policy and, adopting the principle that prevention is better than cure, where a risk can safely be eliminated by using the strategy of a pre-emptive strike, this strategy should be adopted.

The basic principle of the pre-emptive strike is deliberately to bring an issue into the open, set out the facts clearly and in so doing make sure that one has dictated the perspective from which the issue is to be viewed. Assuming that one has a strong case, such action will result in any future debate being won before it has even been entered into.

The danger, and there is a danger, is not so much in facing the main issues but in drawing the attention of fringe activists to the issue and precipitating a 'knock on' problem after the original debate. The major advantage is that no opportunity is provided for false information, which could create a totally false impression. We have seen earlier that reputation is a function of perception and may be only peripherally related to reality. Establishing the truth can be a long and difficult process once false impressions have been formed.

The pre-emptive strike need not be equated with living dangerously. Indeed, if it involves a discernible level of risk it probably should not be employed unless the perceived area of reputation risk is so strong and so likely to develop into a direct threat that it outweighs consideration of any risk resulting from immediate action. There are, however, times when the potential risks involved in acting are negligible whereas the risks involved in sitting tight are considerable.

Once again it is helpful to consider examples and here I shall use fictional cases which closely parallel real events.

A company, knowing that it will be forced into factory closures and redundancies in some 12 months' time, sets out its plans and the reasons well in advance, discusses these with the unions and involves them in a joint plan of action to minimise damage to the individual members of the work force. (This is probably just plain good management but the number of companies in these circumstances which play their cards close to their chest and finish up with union troubles and a reputation as a callous employer are too frequent to attempt to list.)

A company which uses large quantities of packaging manufactured using CFC gasses and sells direct to the consumer has plans to phase out its use over a two year period but cannot do so immediately. The company publicly announces its plans and timetable, with clear demonstration that this is the shortest practicable period. In doing so it eliminates the risk of being targeted by environmental groups and possibly boycotted at any time during the phase-out period.

In both these cases the fictional companies concerned have a fair case to make. This really is crucial if the pre-emptive tactic is to be adopted. With hindsight, it is often easy to see where a decision to pre-empt possible trouble would have been effective but it is far less easy at the time.

Barclays Bank suffered quite seriously during the 1970s from being branded as a bank with substantial South African investments and lost a significant number of customers as a result – particularly among the student population who, because of their long term earning potential, are a prime target group for banks.

In fact, Barclays were far from being the only high street bank with investment in South Africa. But because they were targeted first and because they reacted slowly they, among all the clearing banks, were the only ones to suffer. This would have been a perfect case for pre-emptive action, revealing the degree of investment, putting it in the context of investment by other organisations including the other clearing banks and showing a forward plan to reduce this area of investment, something they eventually did anyway. But it would have been a foolhardy RRM manager who recommended such a course at the time.

Indeed every time one sees a business engaged in fence-mending and setting the record straight on issues of the type discussed here, it is clear that pre-emptive action would have been a good course. What one does not see, however, are the occasions when no pre-emptive action was taken and events proved this to be the right decision.

Incidentally, in looking at the sort of decisions which may be involved in eliminating reputation risk, it starts to become very clear why I have argued earlier that the overall responsibility for an RRM programme cannot possibly be a middle management responsibility but must have a major board level strategic input.

SUMMARY

The first step in RRM, once reputation risk areas have been identified, is to attempt to eliminate all unnecessary risks. Some risks can be eliminated by the introduction of simple procedures which will avoid dangers from poor internal communication – Tower of Babel Risks; some risks can be eliminated by change in business practice when commercial advantage does not balance degree of reputation risk exposure, i.e. The Unbalanced Equation, and some risks can be eliminated by utilising the pre-emptive strike, but this tactic is a double-edged sword and must be approached with caution.

'AT THE COALFACE'
Issue management within a multi-national context

Simon Taylor

The cliché that we now live in a global village is increasingly true in the field of crisis and issue management. A problem arising in a little-known foreign country, in a far away land of which you may know little, could easily destroy your corporate or brand reputation. Even in this case however, where specific planning may not always be possible, there are steps that you can take to limit the damage once it occurs, and to ensure that you are as well prepared as possible. Everything that follows has actually happened, although the names and situations have been changed in order to protect the guilty.

INTRODUCTION

Many senior managers are now in the position of working within the context of a broad-based international conglomerate, based overseas. You may be the general manager of the UK division, dealing in a relatively limited product range from within all those produced by the parent company around the world.

In the UK market, however, you may be a very significant player, and this is where the conflicts sometimes arise. As far as MegaBucks Inc in Detroit or Osaka is concerned, you are turning in good figures for the UK market, but there is no need for you to be privy to the corporate planning decisions that are going on in other sectors within the corporation. It is here that a large landmine could be being carefully constructed, which could explode your market.

The trigger is frequently the international environmental and human rights movements. The environmental movement is now highly sophisticated and extends throught the world. This movement has realised that in order to achieve its ends, it can hit corporations where they are most vulnerable, in the high street.

The consumer boycott is a nightmare for any FMCG brand. It not only hits at sales, it undermines consumer faith in the reputation of the brand and of the company that is selling it. In addition, the stores are not too keen on having pickets outside their doors, undermining their sales and reputation.

Linking a consumer brand or franchise with the actions of the parent corporation has been seen in the UK in the cases of Barclays' and Shell's involvement in South Africa. In the case of the Lynx campaign against the fur trade, a whole industry has been attacked. Regardless of the impact these and other campaigns may have had, they have generated publicity which the companies involved could have done without.

THE PHONE CALL

Most crises begin with a phone call, in this case from a sales manager in Scotland. Imagine that you are the marketing director of the UK FMCG division of a major US multinational. You have a range of consumer products that are either the market leader or in the top three within their own markets. Your sales manager has just phoned to say that Tesco has been on the phone to tell him that there are pickets outside all their Edinburgh stores, handing out leaflets saying that your company is destroying millions of acres of tropical rainforest in South East Asia. You know nothing about this.

It is 9.00am, so with the time difference, you have another four hours to wait before you can phone US HQ head of Corporate Affairs who's first response is 'How the hell did those greens get to hear about it!'.

You gather that there may be some truth in what the activists are saying.

On examination, it appears that the Corporation were investigating the **possibility** of establishing some plantations for raw materials, in an under-developed part of South East Asia. The corporation had come in for opposition from local environmentalists, but had not thought them worth taking seriously, nor had they thought it worth telling the rest of their operations around the world. The environmentalists, together with human rights activists who opposed the regime in the country in question, had alerted environmental groups around the world, using 'Greenet' the world-wide database used by Greenpeace, Friends of the Earth, WWF and other groups. In this way, every Green activist in the world could have access to the issue within hours.

THE THREAT

The risks to the corporation were significant. In the UK, sales of £1/2m per day were at stake in the short term together with long term damage to the corporate and brand reputations. The stores were likely to become hostile towards the company because of the bad publicity the boycott was having. Because of the diverse nature of the green movement in the UK, new 'outbreaks' could flare up at any stage.

In the US, the corporation had major manufacturing facilities as well as retail product distribution. If US consumer and environmental groups picked up the story, then huge damage could be inflicted on them. Around the world they had manufacturing operations in a wide range of countries, in all of which they wanted to be seen as good citizens.

THE RESPONSE

In the initial stages, it was impossible to communicate to the pressure groups, the stores, consumers or the media, simply because the company did not really know what the situation was in South East Asia. In addition, they had not prepared a means of communicating under hostile circumstances. All their PR efforts were brand and trade orientated, none of the senior management team had been through aggressive media training. It was at least two days before the company was in a position to start responding effectively to the problem.

By this stage, a response programme was put together which identified the problems the Corporation was facing. These were:

- a need to respond on the source core issue, i.e. what were the facts of the situation in South East Asia;
- to recognise that although currently localised, because of the world-wide links of the environmentalists, the issue could flare up anywhere in the world where the corporation operated;
- to understand the nature and the motives of the groups who were opposing the project;
- in response to this the corporation established a small team based in the UK, including UK staff, US HQ staff and consultants, whose task it was to respond to the problem.

The UK siting of the team was very important. It added a sense of urgency to US HQ staff by putting them on the front line and ensuring that they understood what the UK staff wanted. The UK was well situated from a time zone point of view, being able to take to both Asia and the US. Finally the UK proved to be vital in dealing with the media and the pressure groups.

All the international media are accessible in the UK, and the BBC World Service played a particularly important part, as they had picked up the story in Asia, and were likely to rebroadcast it world-wide. Both Greenpeace and Friends of the Earth have their World headquarters in the UK, so it was easy to contact, and talk to the major players.

• Accurate information was gathered on the South East Asia project.
This included finding out from the local manager that the site was *not* tropical rainforest. In fact it had once been forest, about fifty years ago, but had been farmed since and was now derelict scrubland. The manager was flown to London, together with video-tape showing the real state of the land, so that he would be available for interviews. In addition, experts were identified who could act as advocates, if required, supporting the development.

• Extensive research was undertaken on the motives of those opposing the project.
Detailed profiles of the pressure groups and their key individuals were prepared, so that company representatives were really well briefed before meetings. We also prepared an analysis of the journalists who were likely to cover the story, together with their past coverage of related issues.

It became clear that the real issue was a political rather than an environmental one. Local human rights groups opposed to the regime concerned were seeking to stop any major investment in the area, and to oppose the Government's development plans. They had deployed environmental arguments against the proposal, which they had circulated to the environmental pressure groups. Understanding this brought about a change in the strategy of response.

• The environmental pressure groups were reassured, and the real political issues were addressed.
Meetings were held between the leading environmentalists, in order to answer their concerns in an open manner. Pre-briefing and rehearsal were crucial to the success of this. The outcome was that the environmentalists agreed, in the light of the evidence, to 'down grade' the issue from active campaigning to monitoring, to ensure that the corporation did as it said it would.

Half the battle was won, in that the environmentalists were largely dealt with. The problem now faced was that of political opposition, as the project was being turned into a flagship for a rather unpleasant regime. It was clear that the corporation in its planning, had not taken the political dimension sufficiently into account, and it was realised that this could have a serious impact in all the western countries where they operated. In view of the pilot and investigative nature of the project, the corporation decided to withdraw.

LESSONS FOR THE FUTURE

It might be said that the corporation failed, in that it was forced to withdraw as a result of outside pressure. The truth is that it failed because it did not do enough initial research. Had it had done so, then it is likely they would not have started the project.

If a bad decision has been made, then nothing is gained by trying to defend it for its own sake. As it happened, the corporation was able to establish good links with environmental pressure groups, because they were able to show how they *did* take the environment into account in their international planning.

A wide range of valuable lessons were learnt.

- A basic communications plan for hostile situations must exist. Senior spokespeople must have had some media training.
- A multinational company must realise that issues will be multinational as well, and be prepared to involve others from around the world, at least in monitoring consumer and political pressures that may cause problems elsewhere.
- Modern communications means that pressure groups can circulate their story to the world within hours. Corporations must be prepared to respond as quickly.
- Establish the facts, tell the truth, and *show you care*!
- Environmental and other pressure groups are better at news management than most corporations. They deal in people and emotions rather than assets and profits.
- Make sure that you know the real background and motivations behind the issue. It is only then, that you can attack the root of the problem.
- If you *are* going into a difficult area, prepare in advance. Many of our problems were caused by the fact that no position or background papers were available. It took many valuable days to gather the data that was required to solve the problem.

- Monitor the situation, even after you believe that you have dealt with it. In this case, we satisfied the national and international organisations, but local groups who had got hold of the information, frequently initiated actions on their own, and had to be responded to.

CONCLUSION

The client got off lightly in this. The real impact, as it is in many cases, was that it was so shocked at how unprepared it had been that it implemented a world-wide issues audit. This audit covered environmental, political, ethical, and work practice issues. Response programmes were then drawn up in the light of the audit's findings. In too many cases, organisations only take issue and crisis managements seriously when it is too late. Effective preparation, together with an understanding of the non-commercial factors that have an impact on organisations, can at least ensure the possible response that any individual situation will allow.

Simon Taylor is an independent communications consultant specialising in communications strategy and crisis and issue management of organisations. He was previously Strategy Director and Head of Corporate and Public Affairs at Ogilvy & Mather PR London, and head of the Corporate and Public Affairs Group at Grayling.

9 TIME – THE CRUCIAL ELEMENT

Elimination of reputation risk will shorten the list of perceived risk areas, but it will not remove it completely. It will leave you with a range of potential threats to the business, some of which will be fairly well defined and others of which can only be categorised in terms of the broad area into which they will fall.

In a perfect RRM programme it will be from this less well defined area that full blown crises will come, if they are to come at all. It is possible to prepare for handling such crises such as those brought about by random consumer terrorism or by a physical disaster but it is not possible to manage them or deflect them in advance within the RRM programme.

It is, however, possible to manage potential threats where these can be well defined. The critical consideration here is time. If there is a lapse of time between the onset of a potential problem and its arrival as a full blown crisis, then there is the possibility of managing the risk, (ideally of heading it off) before it develops. At worst, full damage limitation action will be started in the full knowledge of what will be involved.

Time is the constant enemy of the reputation risk manager and a great part of an RRM programme is dictated by the recognition of this simple fact. When one is in the midst of a crisis, the speed with which one can react is vital. Carefully built up reputations can be destroyed in a matter of hours. Timescales are longer when one is looking at risks which may develop into threat and then into crisis but the same principle applies. Effective management of the risk and effective damage limitation will depend on the speed of reaction and the degree to which one can remain ahead of developments.

There is a great deal which can be done both to extend the amount of time available to deal with risk and to make sure that that time is utilised to the best effect. The techniques discussed in this chapter form the backbone of the day-to-day operation of an RRM programme and may prove critical to success. For the simple reason that, much of the time, these activities are day-to-day, there is a practical danger that they will be allowed to slide and become carelessly managed. It is important to guard against this eventuality and it may well be worthwhile building in the occasional spot check to the management of these activities solely to ensure that they are kept up to scratch.

EARLY WARNING SYSTEMS

The most obvious and straightforward way in which the RRM manager gains time in which to act is through early recognition of potential danger areas. Implementation of early warning systems is an obvious, but too often ignored, activity which will serve to ensure that one knows early, or in advance, where trouble is likely to come from and, frequently, what form that trouble is likely to take.

Monitoring

A thorough system of monitoring is a prerequisite for obtaining early warning of potential risks. Just where the main thrust of such monitoring should be concentrated will be determined by what risk areas have previously been identified in the risk assessment exercise. There are likely to be particular issues and areas which are very business specific. There are also general areas which will be common to all businesses of a reasonable size.

- Media monitoring needs to be carried out intelligently and readers need to know what they are looking for – taking out a clippings service which picks up mentions of company names and products, plus its main competitors, for instance will not be adequate. Reading needs to be issue orientated and to cover national and business press, the main trade journals in a business area, specialist publications dealing with perceived risk areas (e.g. environment, union newspapers, local press etc.) and specialist newsletters. The last of these can provide extremely valuable early information on developments and trends at a very specialist level. They can also be the first place where a crisis surfaces, specialising as many do in investigative journalism.

- Governmental monitoring is complicated and it is usually far too late to spot an issue when it has already surfaced into the public arena whether this be in the form of The House of Commons, The House of Representatives or the European Parliament. If possible Government legislation is seen as a potential area of major risk it may be worthwhile making use of the services of specialists in the field both for monitoring and, when necessary, lobbying.

- Industry Groups have the great advantage of a disparate membership, all of whom are potential information sources and, normally, a secretariat with a responsibility to keep a permanent eye open for issues which will affect the industry.

- Special interest groups may be a source of potential risk and, where this proves to be the case, it can be valuable to monitor their activities and attitudes. It is also normally of value to get close to, and open a dialogue with, such groups to share concerns and deflect difficulties which arise from misunderstandings. Typical of such activity would be the relationship between the various conservation groups and any company whose business involves development of extensive engineering works. Or liaison with disability groups by a restaurant chain over access facilities (a major issue in the USA with its strong disabled lobby and likely to become of increasing importance in Europe).

None of these monitoring activities, nor the monitoring of other special areas dictated by specific perceived risk for a business, is driven by reputation risk alone. For the most part they will already be taking place to some degree as part of the running of any substantial business. What is important is to make sure that this monitoring is being utilised to the benefit of RRM.

In order to ensure that this is happening, two important things need to be done. Firstly it is vital that everybody in a position to carry through such monitoring – PR department and consultants, library information service, representatives on trade bodies, Parliamentary contacts, customer relations department, etc. – is made fully aware of the reputation risk dimension to what they are doing and is fully briefed on those areas of risk exposure which have been identified. Secondly there must be a means by which anyone who spots what might be an early warning sign can get the information quickly and accurately into the right hands. In effect this means that the RRM manager, or one of his or her staff, must be responsible for co-ordinating input from the appropriate monitoring sources and for regular chasing and updating of such inputs.

Monitoring is of little value if the results of such work are not used to inform but lie dormant in the monitor's background information file. Monitoring is of diminished value if it is not carried out with a full understanding of what to look for. Monitoring is also of diminished value if the results are not made available to everyone who may have a use for them, and RRM is an important user of such information.

Forward events

There will be areas of reputation risk exposure which can be clearly identified well in advance and can be planned and prepared for in advance. In some cases, it may even be possible to start to manage these areas in advance. Such risks may be identifiable known events which will occur as a result of (a) advance knowledge of company activity, or because of (b) known external events, or (c) an identifiable cyclical pattern.

Examples of each of these events where there is clear forewarning are:

a. The timing of wage negotiations which are known to be potentially tough and rancorous and with a strong possibility of industrial action.

b. Pre-knowledge of a planned issue of public information. A specific example of this in the UK was the Government's issue of the COMA report which was extremely unfavourable to sugar and which the industry took steps to nullify well in advance of its publication (with only a limited degree of success). Another example occurs virtually every month with the issue of the consumer magazine *Which?'* when there is almost always at least one company whose products or services are panned. The editorial schedule and likely content of such reports are almost always accessible to concerned companies well before publication.

c. In the UK, the inevitable public outcry about appalling rail services which occurs at the onset of winter, when difficult operating conditions combine with staff absenteeism and cold carriages infuriate travellers who are already wet and cold. (With its present monopoly British Rail can largely afford to ignore this, and does, but would have to behave rather differently in a competitive environment.) A rather less politically charged example, again in the UK, is the way in which the established cycle of boom and bust in the housing market puts pressure on building societies not just to manage finances but also to manage the potential reputation risk in the human misery terms of repossessions.

Such areas of risk to reputation are known in advance and a regular review of this forewarned 'calendar of risk' provides additional time to make detailed plans and to prepare the ground for dealing with the situation when it arises.

High probability risks

While not strictly predictable in the sense that they can be included in a 'calendar of risk', there are certain types of risk to reputation which are of such a high level of probability that one can assume that they will develop and will do so in a reasonably short timescale. Such high probability risks may even represent recurrent problems. In such cases, the development from risk to threat can be planned for in some detail in advance, particularly as there will normally be a fairly precise knowledge of the form into which situations are likely to develop.

Examples of this type of risk might be:

- A company with continuing pollution control problems, possibly at a number of separate sites, where it can be anticipated with some degree of certainty that there will be occasions, all be they minor, where systems will fail or underperform.

- A car manufacturer with a wide range of models and a policy of seasonal modification and new model introduction can reasonably anticipate that there will be recalls for adjustment or part replacement on occasion.

- A travel company operating large numbers of overseas package tours can anticipate with a high level of probability problems from flight disruption in high season and/or from inadequate facilities at new destinations – each with the potential to blow up into something more serious than routine operating problems.

Where risk can be identified with this degree of probability and accuracy then it can be absorbed into the early warning system. Detailed plans and procedures can be installed and, as part of the RRM programme, steps can be taken to ensure that there is no escalation to a level at which the threat to reputation can no longer be controlled.

The trained observer

The fourth way in which risk may be identified in advance is less formal and is a result of haphazard information pick up. This may be through noticing some relatively obscure comment during general reading; It may be the result of a chance conversation; it may be because one sees the incidental significance of some event which would not normally be seen as a mainstream threat.

It is remarkable how often the first sign of trouble on the horizon is spotted in this way and how often one can look back on a developing problem and realise that the clues were there but were not recognised before it became obvious that a problem was developing.

Although it is not really possible to formalise this type of early warning, it should not be ignored. There are no rules which can tell you how to recognise these pieces of random information, but there is an attitude of mind which makes it more likely that the signs are spotted. The phrase which probably best describes what is meant here is one borrowed from the world of radical politics and is 'consciousness raising'. The greater the extent to which one is aware of the importance of reputation risk the greater the chances of the relevance of certain random information being recognised.

Given a formal recognition and implementation of RRM as a discipline, a significant level of consciousness raising will already have been achieved amongst those with a connection to the programme. Given the formal systems created to make sure that monitoring activities have an input to the RRM programme, there will be channels by which information gained in a random way can reach the right ears.

In all of these ways the formal implementation of RRM will give a business time to deal with perceived risks to reputation and, used properly, this time will mean that such risks do not develop to crisis proportions.

A point worth remaking is that the aim of an RRM programme is to avoid crises. The programme is at its most intense when engaged in the high profile activity of handling the unavoided crisis, 'managing the unthinkable' as it is sometimes described, and this is when its value is most clearly seen. When it comes to contributing to the health of a business, however, the procedures carried through to eliminate and forestall crises may well make the greater contribution.

SUMMARY

Time is of major importance in RRM and an important part of any RRM programme is to take action which ensures that one has an early awareness of risks which are developing into threats.

Monitoring of all relevant information sources will be of value *only* if:

a. everyone carrying out any form of monitoring has a clear idea of what they are looking for;
b. there are channels to ensure that information which is identified is fed back to the RRM function.

Known forward events can provide a 'calendar of risk' which provides pre-warning and valuable planning time.

Known high probability risk areas can be planned for in some detail and can be treated largely like known forward events.

Random information can be an extremely valuable source of early warning but only if the same two conditions apply as for monitoring and if a 'consciousness of risk' has been achieved.

10 PREPARATION AND EARLY ACTION

There is not a great deal of point in attempting to win time through early identification of reputation risk unless this time is utilised intelligently. Essentially the aim of all action taken will be to control the situation. Without control one is perpetually reacting rather than acting and without control events are managing you – you are not managing events.

A characteristic of crisis management is that, by definition, one starts from a position in which control of events has been lost. A great part of the preparatory work which is put in to crisis management planning is designed to ensure that the initiative can be regained as rapidly as possible. This should not be a problem when managing risk. When reputation risk that is still developing into direct threat has been identified in advance, then control does not have to be lost. A combination of early initiatives and pre-planning for future action should enable one to stay ahead of events, to hold the initiative and to ensure that one remains in the area of managing reputation risk, not managing crisis.

The two main elements of retaining control are taking the initiative and being prepared. For all the types of developing and anticipated threats which were looked at in the last chapter, a combination of initiative and preparedness will normally be required to make sure that a situation is kept under control. However, taking the initiative does not have to mean rushing in at the first sign of trouble. It means taking carefully planned action appropriate to the particular situation. This may well mean taking, or appearing to take, no action at all. There is a huge difference between remaining in ignorance of a steadily developing threat and maintaining a close monitor on developments while waiting to act against a prepared plan, should this prove necessary.

The dangers within an RRM programme of adopting an unnecessarily high profile and needlessly exposing one's business to risk through pre-cipitous action are such that they really do justify a brief digression from the main themes of this chapter. This will, I hope, ensure that the proposed strategy of tackling risks early is not taken as an exhortation to foolhardiness.

AVOIDING THE FRONT LINE

The purpose of RRM is not to win any great victories or to win any medals. It is quite simply to protect a business' reputation against whatever threatens it. To pursue the military analogy further, it is the job of the RRM manager to avoid battle if this can be done and, if battle must be joined, to bring the business out of it with minimal damage by whatever means is most effective.

The fact that there may be occasions where battle cannot be avoided and where the best strategy to minimise damage is out and out aggression, and the fact that in other areas of his or her responsibilities the RRM manager may need to pursue a quite different approach, should not be allowed to mask the fact that, within RRM, intelligent cowardice is the preferred tactic.

In practice this means that, whenever it is possible, directly involving a business in a risk threatening situation should be avoided. Of course, much of the time this simply is not possible and when one is in a full blown crisis it is never possible. When involved in management of developing risk there are frequently times when it is possible to do, or not do, things in a way which minimises the degree of direct exposure.

Every situation is unique and, beyond the general principle of minimising direct involvement, there is no hard and fast set of rules. There are, however, a number of questions which one might ask oneself before leaping into precipitate action and which might prove helpful.

Will allowing the situation to develop further before acting materially affect my ability to control events?
If the answer is 'no' then monitor but do not act. Potential threats often do not develop further.

Is this something which can be handled through my trade association?
If the answer is 'yes' then this must be the preferred route by which to take action.

Is this a specific threat to my business or is it a threat to other business areas?
If the answer is 'a number of industries' then, again, a trade association may be the best channel for action or, if this is not appropriate, a consortium of

interests working together with no single firm being uniquely identified with the issue involved.

Is it possible to handle this properly through a third party, providing suitable briefing and support material?
If the answer is 'yes' then this should be considered but not if it appears devious or underhand. Providing data to an MP with a known interest in a particular area, for example, will normally be perfectly reasonable, this is not done secretively and the MP is not offered any special inducement to act as a spokesperson without declaring an interest.

Does the issue concerned effect a single aspect of the business and, if so, can that aspect be isolated from the business as a whole?
If the answers are 'yes' and 'yes' then this should be done. Examples might be where a potential problem is confined to an operating subsidiary, a geographically specific location, a specific brand etc.

To return to the main theme of discussion. Risks which are recognised early can be planned for and controlled. Once a risk develops towards becoming a threat, there are a series of issues which need to be raised and appropriate action to be taken where necessary. These are:

a. Reappraise the initial decision to allow this risk area to stand and be managed. This decision will have been taken at the risk elimination stage of implementing the programme (see Chapter 8). There is a difference in the judgements made about a risk which just may develop into a problem and the judgements about one which has already started to do so. It may be that this is a point which dictates a change in policy. It is also likely that, once early warning signs appear, the scale of reputation risk can be seen more clearly and may be greater than initially estimated.

   If such a change of policy is indicated then decisions need to be taken about when action should be implemented, the consequences of delaying implementation while attempts are made to deflect the problem, and how such implementation should be handled internally and externally.

b. Check that all information on the situation which can, realistically, be assembled has, in fact, been obtained and taken into account. Given that one has time to plan, one also has time to assemble additional relevant facts – provided that this can be done with an acceptable degree of effort and to an acceptable timescale.

c. Check through the outline plans which exist to deal with a risk of this nature. Refine them as necessary to meet the specifics of the situation faced and be prepared to modify them as required on a continuing basis as the situation develops.

d. Ensure that everyone who needs to know about the situation is kept fully appraised. This will include members of the crisis management team (see Chapter 14) and others who will have a direct involvement in the implementation of the planned action. This information should be provided on a genuine 'need to know' basis, not least because of the 'Tower of Babel' syndrome which was noted in Chapter 7.

e. Ensure that all necessary support and communications systems are in place and up to date. This will include checking on:
   – Availability of all necessary personnel to carry out relevant aspects of the plan when required. (A major benefit of early identification is that you can work to a known timescale, even determine the timing on occasion.)
   – Currency of all relevant contact lists. These may include media, police, Government or Local Authority departments, other departments or sections of the company, outside consultants to the company, company distributors and retailers etc.
   – Full provision of background and briefing information for internal and external use.
   – Mechanical check on the physical support systems which will normally only be needed in a full crisis management situation but which should be maintained at a level of readiness.

f. Cross check that all elements of the plan which do not come under the control of RRM management are fully in place and that there is complete understanding of what needs to be done and how it fits together. In a great number of cases of RRM operating on threats which have been identified early, the action taken will fall largely or wholly under the control of the RRM manager. In other cases, however, such as a controlled product recall or a factory closure, protecting reputation may not be the first management priority, nor may it be the most extensive or complex part of action which needs to be taken.

g. When, and only when, these issues have been dealt with, either by acting on them or by deciding that they are irrelevant to a specific situation, should the plan be put into action. This may seem an overly cautious approach to dealing with reputation risks which may only be a threat on the horizon. But it is worth remembering that an ill-conceived or poorly implemented plan can, in terms of causing damage to reputation, be worse than no plan at all.

THE PLAN OF ACTION

A glance through the 'At the Coalface' sections of this book will confirm that specific activities carried through to manage reputation risk, or manage the unavoided crisis, are as varied as the risks themselves. Successful implementation of a series of actions will, however, depend on their being carried out with a clear purpose in mind and directed at clearly defined target audiences.

In managing reputation risk, it will be the communications aspects of the issue being handled which are of concern. Although we have seen that RRM may stray over into areas which are not strictly a matter of communications, this has always been in the context of decisions or judgements which are taken on the basis of the need communications of perception yardstick to influence perceptions.

As soon as activity extends beyond 'PR' activity, as with product recall, factory closure etc., there is a danger of the communications aspect becoming neglected. Yet a business' ability to manage reputation risk and successfully to limit damage to its reputation at times of crisis will depend crucially on its ability to communicate the right messages to the right people at the right time.

This question of communications activity being undervalued as part of an overall plan of action normally only arises once a risk has become a well developed threat or when the unavoided crisis has occurred. We will return to it when looking at the crisis management element of an RRM programme (Chapter 13). It is, however, something to keep permanently in mind. Even at a relatively early stage of a developing threat, 'practical' considerations of physical logistics can be given excessive consideration at the expense of activity designed to protect the intangible asset of reputation. It is also worth bearing in mind that failure to communicate properly can precipitate a reputation risk where none existed before as a result of totally uncontroversial activity being misunderstood or misinterpreted.

The prime focus of any plan of action to be undertaken will, therefore, be communications. Although specific actions will vary, such plans will need to address the same general areas and will have a broadly similar structure. There is nothing very obscure about this general structure nor, indeed, about the areas to be addressed. The general pattern is not unique to communications projects but is common to almost any planned activity undertaken in a logical way by any function of any business.

Importantly, early or pre-warning of reputation risk means that time has been won to plan properly and, if necessary, to a fairly sophisticated level. One may wish to draw on management techniques developed for other disciplines including flow diagrams, decision trees etc. but, from the point of view of practical experience, this level of elaboration is usually unnecessary and can be counter-productive by imposing too rigid a structure on a range of techniques which, like it or not, are still as much an art as a science.

The basic structure of an RRM plan to deal with a specific threat to reputation should, allowing for variant terminology, be along the following lines:

Objectives
Set out clearly and precisely and, where possible, in a quantifiable way. You are dealing with a clearly defined situation and you should have a clear idea of what you expect to achieve. Objectives should not be allowed to expand into generalities or 'motherhood' statements.

Target audiences
Define clearly with whom you are communicating. There will be a number of quite distinct target audiences and their areas of interest will not be the same.

Messages
Be absolutely clear from the start what messages you wish to get across. Relate these messages back to the target audiences which have been defined. It is very clear that there may be quite wide variations between different messages and different audiences. For example in the case of a corporate reorganisation, the City will have a very different interest and perspective from the work force.

However, though messages may vary in emphasis they must not be contradictory or inconsistent. (The 'Tower of Babel' syndrome has already been discussed in Chapter 8 and is a permanent consideration in any communications activity.)

Strategy
It is essential to establish an overall strategy if the individual activities to be undertaken are going to represent a coherent whole and be mutually supporting.

Activities

These will be determined by the specifics of the reputation risk faced. For any proposed activity two questions should properly be asked:

Does it relate directly to at least one of the determined objectives?

Does it fall within the overall agreed strategic approach?

Unless the answer to both these questions is 'yes', then the proposed activity should not form part of the proposed programme. Alternatively objectives and strategy should be re-examined.

Timing

We have seen that time is a critical factor in being able to control reputation risk. Maintaining initiative needs to be reflected in the timing of all activity and, although this timetable may well have to be adjusted as the plan develops, it is important to have a timed schedule of events in place from the start.

This type of structured plan will work well for those risks which have been spotted early and the development of which can be foreseen, or for those types of reputation risk which can be scheduled within the 'calendar of risk' mentioned earlier. For those risks which can be reckoned to develop into threats with a reasonable degree of certainty, it is not always possible to plan with the same degree of detail. However for such risks the same pattern should be followed and as complete a plan as possible maintained in readiness and in the knowledge that it can be implemented with minimal difficulty.

SUMMARY

Controlling the situation is critical to successful RRM. Control is maintained by:

- taking the initiative;
- being prepared.

Early warning systems gain time which allows the reputation risk manager to both gain the initiative and plan action in advance. This time may be used to:

- reassess company position;
- amplify information base;
- inform all relevant personnel;
- check and modify plans;
- co-ordinate plans with other disciplines;
- ensure all systems are in place;
- create detailed RRM plan.

The plan of action should cover a number of general areas and be formally structured, although detailed action to be taken will vary from case to case:

- objectives;
- target audiences;
- messages;
- strategy;
- activities;
- timing.

A general principle which it will be helpful to follow at all stages of RRM activity will be to minimise direct exposure for one's business, or to confine such exposure to a limited part of the corporate whole, whenever possible.

11 THE BASIS FOR ACTION

It has already been said that every situation is different and that a precise list of actions which may be taken to deal with a developing reputation risk cannot be set down. It is not, therefore, the purpose of this chapter to attempt to provide any such list of actions or techniques. Instead, I intend to set out some general guidelines which may be of value in deciding on specific actions. These general guidelines may be seen as relevant to all aspects of RRM, including crisis management. Similarly, there are a number of behavioural guidelines contained in the section of the book which deals with crisis management (Chapters 12–15) which may be usefully referred to for RRM as a whole. It is helpful to consider just what RRM is and is not, and just what follows from this in terms of action which may be taken.

What RRM is not is a means by which errors of judgement or practice can be concealed, nor is it a means of hiding dishonest or unethical activity. It is, in short, not about lying. What it is about is presenting the facts in a way which will be most favourable to a business. It is about preventing false information or distorted perspectives, which would be damaging to a business' reputation, from gaining credence. It is about winning acceptance and understanding of a business' point of view.

When a drug company makes false claims about the results of testing which it has carried out on a product with the intention of enhancing or protecting that product's reputation; when a company distorts its accounting procedures with a view to deceiving the City into believing that it has performed better than it has; when a company assures its work force that no redundancies are planned with a view to avoiding industrial action until the last big order before wholesale cuts is completed; then this is not reputation risk management. It is lying.

When a drug company shows the results of its testing programme and mounts a concerted campaign to show how benefits derived greatly outbalance any queries which these tests might raise, (an approach which might beneficially have been adopted in 1991/92 by producers of silicon breast implants); when a company changes its accounting procedures and explains how and why these changes give a truer picture of the company's performance; when a company sets out a plan by which it may be possible to minimise redundancies if the current order commitment is completed on time and if further major orders are forthcoming and, therefore, looks to the work force to meet the first of these conditions; then these approaches may legitimately be regarded as RRM.

The point here is not about ethics but about practicalities. It is no part of RRM to go around looking for problems to air. On the contrary, it is sometimes the job of RRM to discourage such investigation but to have ready a good explanation of how the problem came to be there, just in case. The means used to discourage and explain, however, cannot be dishonest ones, if for no better reason than the fact that this does not work. If a business wants to lie, then it would be absurd to do this through a formalised and managed system. The only chance of such dishonest and dishonourable tactics working would be behind closed doors involving as few people as possible.

The task of RRM activity will, then, normally be to present facts and to do so at the right time, to the right people and in a way which is both convincing and empathetic. (The need to create empathy, or at least sympathy, cannot be overstated. Attitudes are influenced at least as much by emotions as by logic and who is to say this is wrong – the American electorate rejected Richard Nixon for President when he ran against John Kennedy as much on the basis of contrasting styles and appearance as on the basis of any logical examination, and look what happened when they changed their minds later and put him in the White House.)

As we have seen, reputation is a function of perception rather than of reality, although such perception will usually be at least partially based on fact. It is not just the marshalling of the facts and the arguments that is important, therefore. It is the way they are presented, to whom they are presented, and when they are presented. If it was really true that 'the facts speak for themselves', a great number of corporate chief executives and spokespersons have gone through very expensive television training for nothing. But anyone who has watched an untrained and inadequately prepared company chairman totally failing to communicate what he wishes to say to the watching millions will realise that it would have been money well spent.

Actions taken should be based on a thorough knowledge of the facts and a suitable presentation of these facts through the most appropriate channels.

It is also worth remembering that when reputation is at risk, there will often be other interested parties with a similar interest in putting forward arguments but which, in their case, are contrary to the best interests of the company. In instances where a threat to reputation has arisen on environmental questions, on labour relations, on consumer terrorism from a special interest group, or on political correctness of investment policy, a company will often find itself engaged in a public debate.

Even where a crisis has developed in a totally non-political way there will be other parties who have an interest in what is said. For example in the case of an aircraft disaster it will matter very much to the aircraft manufacturer, to the various component manufacturers, possibly to air traffic controllers or airport administration or to the pilots' association how blame is apportioned. Or, to take another example, each time there is a consumer product withdrawal, there will be an interest amongst distributors and retail outlets for the product in how this is handled and communicated to the public. These interests will not always be identical with those of the producer.

Where there is a known conflict of interest then it is critical to make sure that one has a clear, factual case to present and that one utilises all available communications channels to present it. Even where there is a potential conflict of interest, this may turn out to be the action which has to be taken, but, at least initially, there is a critical difference.

Where a difference of interests is a prime contributing influence on a risk to reputation, action should be planned to win any resultant debate by seizing the initiative and mustering the full force of PR to communicate the arguments.

In contrast to this direct conflict of interests, a divergence of interests which results from, but does not contribute to, the reputation threat will normally be among parties who are threatened by the same situation and are, at least potentially, allies.

Where there is a difference of interests resulting from a reputation risk situation but not contributing directly to it, action should be taken, whenever possible, to settle such differences outside the area of public debate.

There is absolutely no advantage in inviting publicity when dealing with a reputation risk except in very exceptional circumstances; i.e. on the rare occasion when a pre-emptive strike tactic is adopted to deliberately defuse a potentially threatening situation by bringing it into the open, and on those occasions when the issue is already in the public arena and there is a requirement to inform, clarify and explain. The general rule for RRM (and this does not normally apply to crisis management) is to handle perceived reputation risks as discreetly and in as contained a way as possible.

This point has already been touched on in Chapter 9 and may be formalised into two further guidelines for general RRM action.

Action should, whenever possible, seek to minimise unnecessary exposure for the business.

Action should be designed to be contained within clearly defined parameters as far as possible.

This approach to RRM – to seek continually to confine risk – is one which follows from everything which has been argued in this book so far. In many ways, the approach embodies the core principle of the discipline i.e. RRM is at least as much about *not* having to manage crises as it is about crisis management.

Caution is, consequently, an inherent characteristic of successful RRM. The entire apparatus of risk assessment, early warning systems, prepared positions, contingency planning, pre-training etc. is part of a prudent approach to the management of risk. When RRM activity moves from these essentially passive activities of watching and preparing, this does not mean that this prudent approach should suddenly be jettisoned. Which gives rise to a further guideline.

Action should always be planned with a clear understanding of all the likely consequences and with any plans for follow up action which might be required already in place.

These last three guidelines should not, despite the near timorous tone which has been adopted in formulating them, be treated as an exhortation to secrecy. On the contrary, once one is acting to limit or manage reputation risk, it is vitally important that everyone concerned is kept informed. When we looked at the form which an action plan might take, two of the sections were 'target audiences' and 'communications messages' and recognition of this needs to be carried through into any action taken. Failing to communicate with any key public while carrying through RRM action is one of the fastest ways to escalate risk.

Action which is not targeted at all key publics should always be supported by further action which covers any gaps.

For the vast majority of cases, actions taken as part of an RRM programme will, as previously mentioned, be communications activities. There is an important role for RRM in influencing and advising on other decisions but the executive action required of RRM will be to inform, explain, and persuade. The pro-active part of RRM is, in other words, very much the same as the PR operation of a business – it uses the same techniques and is probably carried through by the same people.

It is in this similarity, verging on identity, that a danger occurs. RRM is an essentially defensive operation and PR is not. It has been argued that one of the reasons for not placing RRM responsibility within a PR department is that it will become subsumed into the general PR programme, to the benefit of neither. At operations level the same considerations apply. It is important to ensure that proposed action within a plan designed to meet a specific threat to reputation is structured from the perspective of RRM and targeted at that specific threat. The best way to ensure that you do not get drawn away from your main purpose by the allurement of creative, but not fully controllable PR inputs is to make sure that all proposed action ties back firmly to the established objectives and strategy agreed by the RRM management team. The guideline can be taken directly from the comments made on preparing an RRM plan in the last chapter.

Any action must be clearly geared to meeting at least one declared objective and conform to the strategic approach as set out in the plan.

I am aware that the guidelines set out in this chapter are both general and, on the whole, prescriptive. This is, I think, no bad thing. Faced with a specific situation it is possible to come up with specific ideas for actions. In fact one can usually come up with too many ideas when the whole paraphernalia of PR and the communications industry is available. What is important is to select from a range of possible actions those which will do the job effectively and with an absolutely minimal possibility of incurring additional risk.

There will, of course, always be the brilliant response to a particular situation but, by their very nature, such ideas are specific to that situation. Such ideas should always be looked at very carefully before being adopted, (which is not to say that they should necessarily be rejected) because, in general, a policy of 'safety first' is the one to follow in day-to-day RRM.

If this sounds unexciting, well so be it. There is more than enough excitement to go round once reputation risk management moves into crisis management and no thanks to the RRM manager who allows this to happen unnecessarily.

SUMMARY

RRM cannot, and should not attempt to, conceal dishonest or unethical behaviour.

Action should be based on suitable presentation of facts through appropriate communications channels to appropriate audiences.

Action must be matched to pre-agreed objectives and strategies.

Caution is an inherent characteristic of successful RRM.

12 THE ESCALATING CRISIS

When a company finds itself facing a crisis, it frequently happens comparatively rapidly and is accompanied by a good deal of drama. The time-scale in which critical decisions have to be made, action taken and a damage limitation programme put into place can be very short indeed – sometimes a matter of a few hours, sometimes a period of days. However much preparation has been done, nobody is ever really ready for a crisis because somehow, statistical probability or not, one does not really expect it to happen – and if it is going to happen then surely not right now.

Whilst crises may frequently be sudden and unexpected, surprisingly often a crisis builds steadily and can be seen developing with what appears to be an awful inevitableness – like those hurricanes picked up early out over the oceans by American weather forecasters and which may finish up flattening large areas of the coast. When this occurs, it is frequently possible to look back and see that it was not inevitable at all but could have been contained or minimised at various points along the way.

The escalating crisis is normally characterised by a series of failures – failure to recognise the risk early, failure to take effective action once the risk had been recognised, failure to develop a proper plan of action and act on it as the risk developed into direct threat; in short, failure to give proper consideration to reputation risk management. Of course it may be that some form of RRM is in place and simply gets it wrong but, in fairness, this is most unusual if there has been any sort of real commitment to dealing with the problem.

In order to illustrate how the escalating crisis can come about and can result in problems out of all proportion to the original cause I have constructed a completely fictional case history which traces the development of such a crisis and indicates some of the failures which help bring it about. I have tried to make it as plausible as possible but, as far as I know it bears no direct relation to any real sequence of events which have ever taken place.

A company, which we shall call Wardfame Ltd is a major organisation operating mainly in construction, civil engineering and related areas. The company has a large number of government and local authority contracts and, both because of its general attitudes to business and as a reputation building exercise, has made a considerable point of the ecologically sound and environmentally conscious way in which it operates. This promotion of a 'green' face for the company has included extensive advertising and the establishment of various award schemes related to the environment.

Wardfame has a range of business interests and has expanded both organically and by acquisition. Because of its strong land bank and property interests, including several builders' merchants operations in prime urban sites, the company might be seen as a potential target for takeover with a view to asset stripping. Aware of this, Wardfame pursues an active City PR operation aimed at support for the share price, together with a shareholder relations programme.

Amongst its various subsidiaries, Wardfame owns a small, loss making building materials producer, called Tildo, based in the West Country. This operation, acquired as a result of a takeover, has persistent but localised pollution problems due to drainage into the local river, the Dart. Its loss making performance has made investment in improved pollution control systems financially unacceptable to its local management. The company has already been fined once for river pollution and this has been reported locally.

In early April a failure of control systems at Tildo results in a spillage of low toxicity waste into the Dart and a high level of short term, localised pollution. A number of dead fish are found in the river along a four mile stretch downstream from the plant. It is the start of the trout fishing season and the Dart is a fly fishing water. The incident is picked up by the local press and a small item appears on the regional television news programme. Reference is made to Tildo and there is speculation that the plant may be the culprit, given its location and previous track record. Tildo refuses to comment initially, but in response to further press queries issues a brief press statement denying responsibility but saying it will carry out an internal check just to be certain.

Tildo's managing director is invited to appear on a local weekly news round up programme on television to discuss the incident. At this point he contacts the head office PR department to seek advice, knowing that the matter will be covered in the programme whether or not he attends. In line with the company's general PR policy of press co-operation, he is advised to accept the invitation and to use the opportunity to state firmly and clearly Tildo's case as already set out in the brief press statement.

The interview is hostile and the MD's performance disastrous. He has had no TV training, is massively overconfident of his ability to handle a mere local TV interviewer, is poorly prepared with facts for the interview, begins by blustering and finishes up evading questions. He is shown to be telling less than the truth.

Following this media disaster, the Tildo MD again contacts head office PR function and, having berated them for their poor advice in putting him on the programme, tells them to 'get someone down here to sort out the publicity'. The visiting trouble shooting PR man realises that the situation is in danger of getting out of control and calls a rapidly convened press conference with a view to regaining the initiative. The main themes of the press conference are Wardfame's outstanding environmental record, a reiteration that there is no knowledge of any culpability but promise of an investigation, a promise to co-operate fully with the National Rivers Authority (NRA) and an offer, without any admission of liability, to restock the affected stretch of the river with rainbow trout and 'such other fish as may be appropriate'.

Media reaction is, at best, mixed. The continued denial of liability is not taken seriously. The generous offer to restock the river is seen as a guilt reaction and does not receive support from the NRA nor from the fly-fishing club with rights to the water. Neither of these had been previously consulted. Anyway the river is stocked with native brown trout, not rainbows which would be unable to breed in the river. The high profile involvement of Wardfame is not seen as the arrival of a saviour but, rather, moves the story out of a local and into a national perspective. The news story goes national and is firmly linked to Wardfame. News coverage features the environmentally aware corporate advertising counterpointed by pictures of dead trout on the river banks. Outraged fly-fishermen in green waders give articulate interviews to press and television. Environmentalists point out the dishonesty of companies which jump on the green bandwagon but continue to pollute and exploit the natural world. The NRA promises investigation and possible prosecution.

At this point, the story is given a further boost by the actions of a small militant conservation group which stages a publicity stunt/photo opportunity by tipping a lorry load of rotting fish on to the doorstep of Wardfame's London headquarters. An on the spot interview given by the group sales director who has just seen his car covered in bits of rotting fish includes references to 'bearded weirdies' and 'sandal-wearing hippies'.

One of the mainstream conservation groups rushes out a dossier on companies engaged in construction and civil engineering, singling out particular subsidiaries with poor pollution records, and linking these with awards of Government contracts. No-one comes out of this well, as is the group's intention. The dossier is provided for the media and as a briefing document to MPs. Although Wardfame's general record is good, the presentation of selective information in the dossier and the fact that the company is already in the news ensures that there is particular focus on such weaknesses as can be identified in its environmental record.

During question time in the House of Commons, a Minister from the Department of Trade and Industry announces Government plans to 'form-alise the procedures for investigating the environmental track records of com-ies tendering for Government contracts'. A circular from the Department of the Environment advises a similar approach by Local Authorities.

Wardfame's share price falls and there is speculation about increased vulnerability to a takeover. Wardfame's chairman fails to receive his expected knighthood in the following New Year's honours list. The head of PR is fired . . .

It is, of course, all fiction. Yet it is not totally fantastic. Indeed it could have been presented as much worse. No reference was made to the type of failures which can so often add fuel to an escalating crisis when a company has no plan or policy to handle such situations – absence of up to date contact lists resulting in incomplete press briefings; unavailability of key executives when required; misdirected telephone calls resulting in speculative com-ment from people who should never have been asked to speak on the issue in the first place; internal confusion resulting in two diametrically opposed courses of action being pursued at the same time; etc.

The fictional crisis described developed because, at almost every stage, there was a failure to follow the sort of RRM programme which has been set out in the preceding chapters of this book. It is worth picking up where these failures happened.

1 At the initial stage of risk assessment Tildo, with its existing track record of pollution troubles, should have been marked as a potential threat, particularly in the light of the Wardfame Group's focus on environmental excellence as a reputation builder. The level of reputation risk repre-sented by Tildo should have been a factor in deciding on further invest-ment on pollution control or, possibly, closure of the operation.

2 Once the incident had occurred, Tildo's initial actions could hardly have been worse – a half-hearted attempt to keep silent followed by a half-hearted attempt to lie. Given previous experience Tildo should have had a plan to deal with any recurrent pollution problems.

3 The absence of TV training was one factor which meant that the TV interview went wrong, but probably more important was the absence of proper pre-briefing and the MD's lack of factual knowledge. This was a real opportunity to recapture public sympathy by showing what efforts had been made on pollution control, promising a full investigation and offering total co-operation with the NRA and fly-fishing club in reversing any damage which had been done.

4 While it would not have been possible to suppress any link between Tildo and Wardfame, the position taken in publicly making the issue one which Wardfame would solve made it inevitable that matters would escalate and the focus would change. This was an unnecessary direct exposure of the parent company.

5 The chance to make common cause with the fly-fishing club and the NRA was completely lost by ignoring the fact that they were each an important public in their own right. Enemies were created who might have been potential allies.

6 The reaction of the environmentalist groups, both militant and mainstream, would be most unlikely if a dialogue already existed between them and Wardfame. The reputation risk to a company in Wardfame's field and with Wardfame's investment in being seen to be environmentally aware is such that any RRM programme would have flagged up the need for such communications channels to exist.

7 The sales director's comments were mainly bad luck but within an RRM programme, control over who speaks to the media on any aspect of a particular issue would have been enforced. No matter how angry or how senior, a director of Wardfame would have been aware of this, had such a programme been operating.

From this point on the scenario is not sketched out in sufficient detail to draw any real conclusions and, in any event, the company has moved from developing risk all the way to a crisis situation.

Although the scenario is fictional, it is not unreasonable to imagine a similar train of events unfolding, indeed they have with surprising frequency. None of our fictional characters did anything particularly stupid, apart perhaps for the sales director who did not affect things that much anyway. Equally none of our fictional characters did anything particularly intelligent but, mainly, reacted in a reasonably predictable way. The real cause of the crisis was the fact that Tildo polluted the river (and even that might have been avoidable as a result of good RRM). From that point on, it is the absence of any overall strategy or plan of action, the absence of any preparation, the absence of any communications links, in fact the absence of an RRM programme which allowed the development of a crisis out of all proportion to the initial cause.

SUMMARY

This discussion, or piece of fiction, about the escalating crisis has, I hope, served to make two main points:

a. Nine times out of ten the escalating crisis which develops with the inevitability of a hurricane is a myth. It is manageable and containable during, and in a sense before, its development using the standard and intelligently applied approach of RRM.

b. As a corollary of this, the absence of a planned RRM programme means that almost any risk to reputation has a real potential to develop from risk to threat and from threat to crisis.

INTO CRISIS MODE

Over the next few chapters we will be looking at the specific discipline of crisis management although some of the areas discussed apply also to day-to-day RRM, particularly in terms of pre-planning and preparation. The type of crises which we will be looking at come suddenly and, almost certainly, carry with them elements of the unexpected. It is to handle this type of crisis that companies design and implement crisis management programmes.

Crisis management is conducted under pressure, makes massive demands on an organisation's resources, is rarely 100 per cent successful in preventing any damage to a business' reputation and is hugely disruptive to normal business. There is no way that any sane person would wish to be put in the situation of managing a crisis if earlier management of risk could have prevented this.

13 THE FULL-BLOODED CRISIS

If you are working out how to handle a crisis as it happens then you are already in very deep trouble. That at least is the conventional wisdom about crisis management and, in some respects, it is true. It is certainly true if what you are working out is who should be helping with managing the various aspects of the crisis, where you should all be meeting, what telephone lines are available, where the files might be which can provide some background information etc. It is not true if what is being considered are the specific implications of the particular crisis being faced, by a team of people who know what their particular responsibilities are, and who are backed by a full support team and a full range of support services.

Every crisis is different and in every crisis there is the element of the unexpected. There is no system in the world which can manage a crisis by routines alone and no amount of training and preparation can guarantee levels of performance in a real crisis situation. What an RRM programme can do is to ensure that in a crisis the crisis management team is able to concentrate on the key issues without distraction, can make decisions in the knowledge that the structure is there for their speedy and effective implementation, can act with some understanding of the issues involved and with some support aids to decision making, and can act in the knowledge that its members have been prepared to respond to just such an emergency as the one which is faced.

In a crisis it is unlikely that the RRM manager will be the leader of the crisis team. There are often, and quite properly, other more important matters to deal with than questions of the company's reputation. Though it will be how well a business reacts to these reputation needs which will largely determine how far it is permanently damaged by the situation in which it finds itself.

REPUTATION PROTECTION

So far we have been concentrating on management of risks to an organisation's reputation, and even the discussion of the escalating crisis was primarily about damage to reputation. In the case of a sudden, full blown crisis it will almost always be a business' operational response to the situation which will be the first priority. Concern for a company's reputation will, of course, be there but will play a very secondary role in decision processes which may involve matters of safety or health.

The proper order of priority issues in managing a crisis will probably be:

a. preventing any threat to life, health or safety;
b. minimising any distress or avoidable worry to individuals and to the public at large;
c. taking socially responsible action in dealing with issues (e.g. police co-operation in cases of consumer blackmail);
d. protecting the company's commercial interests;
e. protecting the company's reputation.

Apart from feeling that e) will have more long term importance than d), there can be no suggestion that priorities along these lines should be revised to be more selfishly ordered on a company's behalf. Anyway, effective implementation of a), b) and c) are usually a pre-condition for achieving d) and e). Nonetheless, the reason a business exists is to trade successfully – with all the social benefits (employment, creation of wealth etc.) which this implies. It is, thus, just as much a dereliction of duty to fail to take action in protection of the business as it is to fail in any other responsibility.

This concentration on physical and logistic problems can mean that it is the communications aspects of a crisis which may be neglected. But effective communications will be a vital part of the management of the crisis itself. It will also be the success or failure of communications strategies that largely determine how much long term damage a business suffers from a crisis.

The damage to company's reputation will depend upon a series of perceptions among its key publics. Such perceptions will be based not so much on facts as on the degree to which those facts have been successfully communicated. Perceptions which will be critical in this respect are:

• How much care the company had taken to guard against this type of crisis occurring and, consequently, how far the company should be regarded as victim rather than cause of the crisis.
• How effective the company's response to the crisis is.
• What priorities the company is seen to have in its response to the crisis.
• How 'human' is the face of a company in the light of the crisis.

For a business to survive a crisis with its reputation relatively intact, it is not enough to manage a crisis well, it must also be seen to be doing so.

SEIZING THE INITIATIVE

We have discussed earlier how important it is to take and maintain the initiative in RRM activity. If this is important for the day-to-day operation of an RRM programme dealing with perceived risk and possible threat then it is one hundred times more so in dealing with a crisis.

It is virtually certain that a crisis will start with a company having to react to an unexpected situation and with all its responses being dictated by outside events. The longer this continues, the more likely it is that the company will be perceived to be unable to control the crisis and hence be seen to be inadequate and, by implication, culpable.

The first priority of crisis management is to get back in control and this means to start taking actions which are not dictated to the company by events but which are the result of company initiatives. In essence this means getting ahead of events and anticipating developments before they happen. Even where action is, in fact, forced upon the company, if that action is taken before it is seen to be inevitable then the company is perceived to be in control. Consider how a surfer is perceived to be controlling the seas, although, in truth, once he's up and riding a wave he doesn't have too many alternative options. Actions taken to regain control will frequently involve using effective communications techniques. Ensuring that the company is *seen* to be in control will *always* depend on the successful communication of its actions and its position to all of its key publics.

CENTRAL ROLE OF COMMUNICATIONS

The effective management of a crisis will rely heavily on good communications. It will be found that during the crisis it can often become clear that communications activity is serving the double role of helping to manage the crisis and of protecting the company reputation. For example:

If there is evidence of widespread product tampering which renders a consumer product potentially unsafe, it will be important to get the message to the general public that previously bought product should not be consumed. At the same time, further sales through retail outlets will be halted. Issuing the warning is a direct element in controlling the effects of the crisis. The way in which the warning is issued will affect perceptions of the company's reaction to the crisis and, hence, its reputation.

Similarly, establishing hot line information services for relatives and friends of people who may have been involved in the disaster is an essential step in the case of an aircraft crash, accident to a passenger ship etc. The extent and manner of publicising this service will be critical both to the service's effectiveness and to perceptions of the operator's response to the disaster.

This leads to a further point in relation to the interaction between crises and public perceptions which is rarely made, although I believe it is widely understood. This is that it will often be because an issue is in the public domain and because the attention of an organisation's key publics is focused on its performance that it is regarded as a crisis rather than an operating difficulty. In other words, there are numerous occasions where it is the perceived seriousness of a situation rather than the real seriousness which can demand the application of crisis management. Where a food producer identifies contamination in a particular batch of product and needs to recall that batch before any purchaser is put at risk the situation is genuinely serious and will call for rapid and effective product recall. There may be a real health risk to consumers and the gravity of the situation should not be underestimated. It is a situation with the potential to become a crisis but, in itself, will not call for full blown crisis management.

Contrast this with the situation which faced Mars in the UK in 1984 when a group of animal activists, known as the Animal Liberation Front, falsely claimed to have poisoned Mars bars throughout the country. This was a hoax and there was no genuine risk to the public, although Mars could not initially be sure of this. The false claim attracted massive publicity and Mars was involved in total crisis management. (The competence of Mars' performance on this occasion was, incidentally, seen after the event to have enhanced rather than diminished the company's reputation.)

It may be ethically unpalatable but it is a commercial fact of life that an organisation faces corporate crisis only when whatever has gone wrong has impacted on the organisation's key publics or has the potential to do so. To give a further, particularly brutal example, a site accident involving a construction company and causing a number of fatalities at an overseas project in the Third World is unlikely to precipitate a corporate crisis; the same accident, involving the same company, with the same death toll in central New York might very well do so.

The level and nature of the perceptions of key publics are a factor in the nature of a crisis as well as a consequence of the crisis. How these perceptions are formed and what these perceptions are will depend, almost entirely, on how effectively a company can communicate with these key publics. It is the job of the RRM manager to take responsibility for the communications aspects of crisis management; it will normally also be his or her responsibility to ensure that an organisation is prepared for handling crisis. This responsibility will extend beyond the purely communications function. The activities which need to be carried through by the RRM manager logically extend to the provision of support for the crisis management team in addition to membership of that team. There is no absolute rule that this should be the case and it would, in theory, be possible to separate the role of crisis preparation and training from that of RRM but, in practice, this would be a potentially confusing and unbeneficial division of responsibilities.

CALMNESS THROUGH PREPARATION

In crisis mode, damage limitation will be the major concern and time is critical. There are rarely any second chances on decisions and they will have to be made under the pressure of the gravity of the situation, under the pressure of time and developing events and against a background of multiple calls for one's attention. If one is to function effectively in this environment the single most important consideration is calmness. Rational judgements and measured responses are not the results of frenetic energy but of careful and informed consideration. Achieving this will depend only partly on the abilities of the people managing the crisis to perform in this way and under these conditions. It will be more important to ensure that the company's potential capability for crisis management can be realised when it is needed. To do this pre-preparation is vital and should cover as a minimum:

- trained crisis management team;
- an 'all you need to know' crisis manual;
- individual manuals/check lists for team members;
- equipment and physical support systems;
- full support information/decision aids.

Each of these deserves discussion in its own right and the next few chapters will deal with them in more detail.

SUMMARY

Every crisis is different. Each has an element of the unexpected.

Reputation is unlikely to be first priority in a crisis.

Damage to reputation will depend on perceptions. The perceived seriousness of a situation – rather than the actual seriousness – can demand application of crisis management.

The reputation risk manager should take responsibility for communications within crisis management.

The priorities of crisis management are;
– to regain control;
– to remain calm.

'AT THE COALFACE'
State of alert!

Michael Regester

The black bleeper normally fixed to my belt was, on this particular evening, lying on top of my desk in my study at home. At twenty minutes to nine my youngest daughter came charging through the house saying: 'Dad, your bleeper is making a funny noise'. I rushed into the study and saw that the bleeper was giving me a 'Level Two Emergency' warning. I knew exactly what had to be done. I grabbed the 'black bag', ran to my car, and as I started the journey from Cambridge to Knightsbridge in London, I used the car phone to begin calling out members of the emergency response team. The reaction was the usual one. 'This is just another exercise, isn't it Mike?'

'No, this time it's for real,' I said. 'Please make your way to the office as quickly as you can and I'll meet you there'.

The office in question belonged to Elf Aquitaine UK (Holdings), parent company for Elf's exploration activities in the UK sector of the North Sea. That week my company had been on standby duty for the company's external relations department, headed by Ann Davis, to provide backup support in the event of an emergency situation developing.

That night, on 22 May 1991, a gale had blown up in the North Sea which was so powerful that a drilling rig, under contract to Elf, being towed by two tugs towards the Shetlands was itself pulling the two tugs backwards. It was clearly a potentially dangerous situation and the sensible decision to evacuate all non-essential personnel was taken. As soon as that decision was communicated from the rig to the Elf office in Aberdeen, it would only be a matter of minutes before news of the evacuation would reach the press located in that city.

Radio hams listen into conversations from rigs and platforms on the VHF channel, just as they do to conversations between airline pilots and airport control towers as planes land and take off, and any hint of trouble is passed on to newspaper offices – in exchange, of course, for a small consideration. It was in this way that news of the Piper Alpha tragedy had first reached the media in Aberdeen.

At the time, Elf maintained only a small operational office in Aberdeen which would be unable to cope with enquiries from the media or relatives of families working offshore. It was agreed, therefore, that in the event of an emergency, any such calls would be transferred to the larger London office, where proper records are also kept and information can be quickly gathered. Elf, like an increasing number of companies, had given a great deal of thought as to how they would communicate effectively to an anxious outside world when faced with a problem offshore. The company realised that the ability to communicate quickly, accurately and honestly was crucial if its reputation was not to risk being damaged after the emergency had been dealt with.

This is where the 'black bag' came in. Company problems have a habit of developing on Christmas Day, at night or on the weekend. In that event, we realised that we would need instant access to telephone numbers and the latest information about the state of the company's offshore operations. All of these were contained in the 'black bag'. Other crucial items included in the bag were a mobile phone (with spare batteries), cash and keys to the offices.

By 11pm, emergency response team members had all assembled at Elf's Knightsbridge offices and were being briefed on the location of the rig, the status of the evacuation, where the men were to be evacuated, and what was being done to make the rig secure. Media calls had already begun streaming into the office. A specially designated 'media response room' had been quickly set up with eight telephone handsets operating on a separate number from the main switchboard. This number had been released to the press via the wire services and allowed the main switchboard to remain free for other calls. Similarly, a 'relative response room' had been set up with its own telephones and separate telephone line.

The emergency response teams that I had called on my drive into London were all members of Elf staff, with the exception of my own colleague, Caroline Searle, but were not usually employed by the external relations or human resources departments. They worked for other parts of the organisation and had all undergone intensive training on either how to respond efficiently to media calls or sympathetically to calls from family members. The two techniques are quite different, because of the different demands from each group.

In my experience, one of the most important areas of information that the press require during an emergency is adequate 'background' on what had been going on at the time of the emergency. We had anticipated this and had prepared a 'Fast Facts' reference book so that the team responding to the media could, at a glance, look up details of the company's safety record, the safety record of the offshore oil industry as a whole and a whole host of other relevant information. Equally, we knew that we would need fast access to the names of people on board the rig, which ones were being evacuated by helicopter, and where they were being flown to. All of this depended on computerised information systems being in place and working properly.

As events turned out, the evacuation was smoothly handled and the rig quickly made secure. No relatives phoned the office and by the time they saw breakfast television news and read the newspapers, they had already received calls either from the company or from their own relatives who had been evacuated to assure them that all was well. Media interest came mainly, as might be expected, from the Scottish press and by 2am calls had virtually dried up. Shortly after this time, Ann Davies was able to stand down the teams and a small number of us spent the rest of the night tracking the progress of the evacuation and responding to the few calls that still came in. In the early morning, we put together a final 'it's all over' press release and disappeared into Covent Garden for breakfast.

Media coverage was mainly restricted to Scotland. All reports were absolutely accurate. Two Scottish newspapers wrote to the company and thanked it for its co-operation throughout the night.

From both an operational and communications standpoint, things might have been a great deal more difficult had the company not been so well prepared. As soon as there was a hint of danger, the decision to evacuate the men was taken. Many hours of 'rehearsal' for the call-out teams, thought and planning which went into the procedures, leading to a fast and effective response enabled the organisation to react positively. Many others would not be able to do so because of the prevailing attitude that 'it will never happen to us' – when, of course, one day it almost certainly will.

The key to crisis management is crisis prevention whether the vigilance and preparation is self-motivated or enforced by legislation. In the event of a fire, comprehensive contingency planning and management training can minimise the catastrophe, while a policy of open and truthful communication can reduce damage to corporate and individual reputations.

Assuming that the will to be open and truthful exists, consideration needs to be given to the people and procedures required to transmit fast, accurate information about what has happened; who was involved; what is being done; and, where appropriate, how the company feels about the situation.

Technological wonders like offshore drilling rigs are no more trustworthy than are the human beings who design and operate them. Safety must be as much part of the corporate culture as the profit motive. But so must the readiness and ability to explain what has happened if the unthinkable ever does.

Michael Regester is Managing Director of Regester plc, the only consultancy in the United Kingdom to specialise entirely in issues and crisis management. He is an acknowledged international authority, author and lecturer on issues and crisis management and is generally regarded as having pioneered many of the systems, procedures and training programmes which companies can put into place to handle effectively the communications aspects of crisis situations.

14 THE CRISIS MANAGEMENT TEAM

Dealing with a crisis needs to be a team effort in all ways. A crisis will always disrupt the general run of a company's business and significant numbers of people will be required to implement the range of damage limitation activities which are undertaken as part of crisis management. Management of the crisis will also be a team effort – crisis management is not something that can effectively be undertaken by a chief executive acting alone. The management team, however, needs to be small, and to consist of people who have a clear understanding of what their role within the team should be.

A useful guideline for forming the crisis management team is that *it should be confined to those people who will have a continuous input to the decisions required to manage the crisis as it develops*. This means that there is no need to fill the team with people, however senior, whose main task in a crisis will be to manage the implementation of a decision taken by the management team. Such experts in their fields will, of course, be needed to join the team and provide advice and guidance on their specific area but only while that area is under consideration.

Thus when, for instance, a product recall is being discussed and decided on, the manager responsible for carrying this out will have inputs to the decision process and will have valuable information about the logistics of the operation. However, once the decision to go ahead with a recall is made, there is no further need for the manager to remain within the team and contribute to, say, the form of announcement to be made to the media. Failure to follow this guideline will result in the management team swelling to an unmanageable size and defeating the purpose of creating a tight, well defined team.

It is not possible to be dogmatic about the exact composition of a crisis management team since the ideal combination will vary from organisation to organisation. It may also be the case that the precise make up of the team will be modified depending on the type of crisis faced. For example, a crisis precipitated by industrial action might well dictate the permanent presence of the personnel or industrial relations manager in the managing team; a corporate crisis brought about through events affecting a subsidiary company might require the MD of that subsidiary to be a member of the team, and so on.

THE CORE TEAM

There will, however, be a core membership of any crisis management team which will consist of:

- the company chief executive, acting as chairman and final decision point;
- a second in command for the team, who will also act as the main internal contact point between the team and the company's mainstream management functions;
- the manager responsible for reputation risk (possibly, but not necessarily, corporate relations director);
- a corporate 'guru' – it is difficult to provide a precise term for this member of the team because the exact position will vary from company to company. In the USA it is a role normally described as 'corporate counsel' but, in the UK, this position does not exist very often.

The slightly facetious description of 'corporate guru' is meant to emphasise the fact that this member of the team will normally be a staff officer of the corporation rather than a line manager, and that the role will be to aid and advise on decision making but with little executive commitment. A legal background is strongly indicated, but experience has shown that in situations where a practising lawyer's approach is taken to crisis management, the consequences to reputation are usually disastrous.

It may be necessary to extend beyond this core group but a crisis management team should never exceed six members plus a secretary if it is to remain properly focused. Research into group dynamics indicates that loss of focus starts once a group has more than four members.

MANAGEMENT TEAM RESPONSIBILITIES

The overriding responsibility of the crisis management team is to concentrate on key issues and to direct the action which the company should take to respond to and, ultimately, control the crisis which the company faces. The team cannot confine itself to general decisions, however, and must take responsibility for executive action – even though implementation of such action will normally be delegated. These areas of executive responsibility need to be defined and divided between the crisis management team membership.

Assuming a team confined to the four core members suggested, the areas of responsibility indicated above are, in slightly more detail, likely to be:

Team chairman

- Takes ultimate responsibility for management of the crisis including deciding on the level of crisis, determining priorities of action and allocating corporate resources.
- Acts as the 'face' of the company in dealing with the crisis by being the corporate spokesperson and, if necessary, taking direct personal action on behalf of the company management.

Team No 2

- Controls all interaction between the crisis management team and the required support functions within the company.
- Ensures proper information liaison with the mainstream running of the company, and ensures that the normal functions of the company continue to operate as far as possible, during the crisis.
- Takes responsibility for the maintenance of a continuous log of events during the crisis and, in conjunction with the reputation risk manager, conducts any necessary post mortems.

Reputation risk manager

- Takes responsibility for all external communications activity carried out by the company including the issue of press releases, handling all media enquiries, arranging broadcast participation.
- Provides continuous update information for the team on the development of the crisis, including, as far as possible, external perceptions of management performance.
- Manages the support functions of the team itself. (This dual type of responsibility is discussed further below.)

Corporate guru

- Carries through all formal official external contact, police, security insurance etc.
- Provides, or ensures the provision of, informed advice on all legal aspects of the crisis.
- Acts as 'keeper of the corporate conscience' by maintaining awareness within the team of the established corporate priorities and ethics. (More often needed than might be imagined when harassed executives are facing the need to take pragmatic decisions under pressure.)

MAIN SUPPORT TEAM

Additional members may be co-opted into the team as the situation demands and there will be certain functions which need to be on immediate call to the crisis management team. These will normally be covered by:

personnel/industrial relations director;
public relations manager (when not already covered by RRM);
operations/manufacturing director;
product recall director;
sales director
marketing director.

All of these will want to join the crisis management team – they will want to contribute, join in decision making processes, essentially they will want to be in the front line when the going is tough. This attitude, admirable though it may be in the normal running of a company, is not helpful in crisis. The ability of the crisis management team to concentrate on key issues depends on it being protected from extraneous influences. Non-essential members of the team should be ruthlessly excluded from full time participation and only involved where there is a direct need for their expertise.

Where there is an outside crisis management consultant, then that consultant should be a member of the crisis management team, but this should only be done where such a consultant has been part of the continuous process of preparing for crisis and directly involved in the RRM programme. Where outside expertise is called in as a reaction to the crisis and in order to strengthen the company's capacity to manage the situation in which it finds itself, then it is normally much more sensible to utilise the outside consultant's expertise as an adviser to the team and not as a full member of it.

Use of consultants is discussed in more detail in Chapter 20, but essentially the consideration has to be that all core members of the team must be thoroughly steeped in the company culture and have an overall awareness of general company issues. A 'visiting fireman' consultant will know about crises but there simply is not the time to provide a full background briefing on the company. (The exception to this is when a company realises that it is not managing a crisis well and calls in help to rectify a worsening situation. When this happens then outside expertise should be given as much weight as possible.)

The final, and indispensable, support member of the crisis management team will be the secretary. This is an important job and one which should not be underestimated. Although having no part in the decision making process, at the height of a fast moving crisis situation, the degree of unflustered efficiency which he or she can bring to the crisis room can be a major factor in maintaining calm. The log of events, normally the responsibility of the crisis chairman's number 2 but kept by the secretary, is important both in keeping track of events and in reviewing the situation both during and after the crisis.

UNDERSTUDIES

Every member of the team should have an understudy who is fully prepared to fill the role within the team should this prove necessary. People travel on business, get sick, take holidays and one must always assume that when a crisis breaks it will be at the most inconvenient time. Vital time will be lost if the crisis management team cannot start to function immediately. At least one, possibly two, understudies must be appointed for every role and these understudies should be as fully prepared as the first choice members of the team. Crisis management is one skill where learning on the job is not to be encouraged.

CRISIS ROOM

For the team to function efficiently, it needs to operate in an environment in which information is readily available and in which decisions can be swiftly implemented. At the same time, the team needs to be kept away from the frantic activity which a crisis engenders. It also needs to be protected from the hundreds of relatively minor operating decisions which will have to be taken on a running basis. This, effectively, means that the team needs to be physically separated from the functioning of rest of the business. Establishing a properly equipped crisis room which is always available for use when needed is a necessary part of the programme of preparation which will have been put in place by RRM activity.

COMMUNICATIONS CHANNELS

The team may be physically separated from, but must not be out of contact with, the rest of the operation. Making sure that decisions reached by the team are communicated to line management is relatively straightforward. So too is establishing a communications channel which ensures that the team receives any information which it requests. What is more difficult is making sure that any development of importance or any significant request for guidance reaches the team, while at the same time ensuring that low priority information and low level decision making is not allowed to get through and confuse the main issues.

Filtering information and deciding what should be referred to the team is a job of considerable importance and needs to be the ultimate responsibility of a single individual. He or she will, of course, be able to consult with colleagues but if more than one person can feed information into the team or request guidance then, once again, the ability of the team to function efficiently will be impaired by too many diversions. In practice this filtering is not as difficult as it sounds. It is usually fairly obvious what are priority requests or information and it is only the occasional marginal matter which requires judgement. This filtering role can be effectively combined with that of being in charge of implementing external communications activity, with both functions reporting to the RRM manager. It is a role best performed by the head of PR, or his deputy where he is a member of the core team in his role as RRM manager.

THE ACTOR MANAGER

In some ways the role of the reputation risk manager during a crisis can be compared to that of the old style actor-manager in the theatre. He will have assembled the company, arranged the scripts, provided briefing notes and stage directions. He will have been largely responsible for support services – prompt, wardrobe mistress, front-of-house liaison, advertising and promotion. He will deal with the press and provide the answers for box office queries from the public. He will be responsible for fixing rehearsals and for making sure everyone knows their lines. Unlike the actor-manager, however, he is unlikely to play the lead in the play although his part will be a central and important one.

While playing with this analogy, one might also make the point that this is a 'one show only' performance at which no allowance will be made for first night nerves. No mistakes of timing or delivery can be rectified for the next performance. Moreover, the critics will be filing their notices throughout the duration of the play and audience participation will influence development of the plot even as the story unfolds. In the event of a flop, it will be a severely depleted company of players which attempts to mount any further productions.

The serious point to be stressed here is the multiplicity of concerns that RRM must take on board during a crisis and to emphasise that this can only be done if proper preparation and training has already taken place. An additional point is the reminder that the actions taken by the crisis management team have got to be right first time – there will be no second chances – and the capability for doing this will depend largely on being free to focus exclusively on key issues without distraction.

SUMMARY

Dealing with a crisis is a team effort. The team should be confined to those who have a continuous input into the decisions required to manage the crisis as it develops.

The core crisis team will probably consist of:

– company chief executive;
– second-in-command;
– reputation risk manager;
– corporate guru;
– secretary.

Additional members may be co-opted as appropriate but must be excluded from full-time participation.

Each member of the crisis management team must have at least one understudy – possibly two.

The crisis team must concentrate on key issues and therefore needs to be physically separate from the rest of the business.

Selected (important) information must be filtered to the team – probably through the PR function.

15 THE CRISIS MANUAL

The designation of the members of the crisis team, outlines of the responsibilities for members, rules and guidelines for action, checklists, contact lists and any other specific information which will be needed in the event of a crisis should be kept together in a single source document. This document will be the bible for procedures and systems which are put into place as soon as a crisis is identified and will be the single authoritative reference point for crisis management.

The crisis manual will be at the heart of structuring a crisis management programme and the aim should be to make this document sufficiently watertight to cover all eventualities at least as far as responsibilities, systems and procedures are concerned. Having said this, it is clear that the crisis manual should not be a vast and indigestible tome. The last thing that will happen during a crisis is that one starts studying the manual. It should be a document which is readily absorbable by the members of the crisis team as part of their preparation, a basis for training in systems and procedures, and a readily accessible source of check lists and of key contacts.

All members of the crisis team, and their understudies, should have a copy of the crisis manual at home. Although it is excessive to say that they should take it with them wherever they go, the reputation risk manager and the chairman of the crisis team will want to know that a copy of the manual is readily available when they are away from their main office for a protracted period (for example working out of a branch office for a number of weeks).

Members of the crisis team and immediate support staff can reasonably be expected to familiarise themselves with the general procedures laid down in the manual and with the specific sections which relate to their particular responsibilities in being prepared for a crisis, in the event of a crisis alert or during the management of a crisis proper.

This may seem a somewhat hopeful requirement of the members of the crisis team and, admittedly, it does not reflect reality to expect the chief executive of a major corporation to take a copy of the crisis manual with him when leaving for a month's safari holiday in East Africa, for instance. It is not an unrealistic requirement to expect the chief executive to be fully confident that his substitute is both able and prepared to manage a crisis in his absence, and it is no more than reasonable to expect all members of the crisis team, management and support, to be fully *au fait* with the relevant contents of the manual. The fact that this does not always happen is a reflection of the degree to which companies continue to be unprepared for crises through failing to face up to statistical probability rather than an indication that this simple requirement is too much to expect.

The manual is, in itself, no more than a means of pulling together the various elements which have gone into setting up a crisis management system. Moreover, during a crisis it is unlikely to be of much direct value, except as an instant reference source for members of the crisis team who are operating away from the crisis room. Much of the information which it contains will be duplicated within the crisis room – on the day check lists of responsibility for members of the team, up-to-date contact lists with telephone numbers and locations and guideline instructions for handling particular tasks. The crisis room will also be equipped with further information which will not, normally, be included in the manual, such as possible scenario check lists and decision trees. Nonetheless, it is the formal crisis manual which is the tool for ensuring that all the elements which are needed to enable an organisation to act efficiently and effectively at a time of emergency are in place. It is the manual which is used as the basis for training and preparation. It is by insisting on regular updating of all of the information contained in the manual that the reputation risk manager can ensure that systems and information remain in a state of readiness. It is on the basis of the manual that training and testing of crisis preparedness can be conducted, and from this testing the manual itself may in turn be modified.

It is worth looking in some detail at the form which a crisis manual may take. In doing this it will not simply be the manual itself which can be focused on, but he range of matters which needs to be covered in preparation for crisis. One point which comes over very clearly from the consideration of the manual is just how many people need to have some degree of preparation and also how important it is to keep a continuing check that information remains up to date, that support equipment remains functional and that systems remain current. I have had direct experience of an occasion where building work at a company's headquarters meant that the designated crisis room had been reallocated as a staff rest room and all the materials kept in readiness for crisis put into store during the redecoration by the cleaners. No executive could locate them, and no arrangements had been made for the newly defined crisis room to function as such if needed, including no provision for phone links. Fortunately this came to light as a result of an unannounced spot check and not during a real crisis.

There will be variations in style and approach to the format and contents of the crisis manual from company to company. Some companies may choose not to include everything listed here in the crisis manual itself. It may be decided to provide additional, specialist documents for the use of each of the individual members of the crisis management team. It may be decided to hold some of the information which will only be used during a crisis in the crisis room itself and not to include it in the manual.

On balance, it is probably best to include as much as possible in the crisis manual up to the point that it becomes too detailed to allow quick and easy reference and is unlikely to be read through and absorbed by the crisis team and key support staff. There will need to be very precise detailed procedures for product recall, for example, and these clearly should be contained in a separate document and not included as an appendix in the crisis manual – the appendix would in all probability be several times longer than the manual itself. Similarly one needs to decide what degree of detail should be included. Too much detail will make the manual indigestible and difficult to absorb, too little will tend to make it so general as to be valueless.

Although there will be some such variations, every crisis manual will cover much the same areas, Variations will tend to be additions to these core elements, reflecting particular concerns of the company involved. These main elements are:

Overview

It is important that the contents of the manual should be placed in context for everyone who is going to use it. A general overview of what the manual aims to achieve, together with general guidelines about the company approach to crisis, provides such a context. Contents of such an overview should be kept simple and short but should seek to emphasise key points:

- declared corporate priorities at time of crisis;
- the importance of remaining calm, and sticking strictly to guidelines for all personnel involved, including, and perhaps particularly, support staff;
- an exhortation to read, absorb and inwardly digest relevant sections of the manual;
- a guide to usage of the manual itself before and during a crisis.

Allocation of responsibilities

A comprehensive listing by name and position of all members of the crisis management team and designated support staff, together with understudies, is essential. This listing should include all contact information for each individual i.e. work and home telephone numbers, mobile phone, additional contact numbers where a member of the team works from more than one office and any other contact information which may be appropriate.

It may be very important to get the crisis team into action as quickly as possible and speed of contact will be a major factor in this. Where rapid action is required, the team may initially be made up of at least some substitutes and one will need to support the acting team, while at the same time contacting and briefing 'first team players'.

Procedures for invoking crisis

There needs to be a clear set of procedures for invoking a formal crisis situation and these need to be clearly set down. The responsibility for formally putting a company into crisis mode should normally be limited and may be confined to the chairman of the crisis team and the reputaion risk manager, or their understudies acting in their absence.

Without a clear definition of who has the formal right to invoke crisis management there is potential for serious chaos and recurrent false alarms. If the responsibility is spread wider, for example to any board member, then there will need to be a formal requirement that the chairman of the crisis management team and the reputation risk manager are the first two people contacted – bringing control back to the two key players in setting up the emergency team and procedures.

An intermediate position between normal activity and full crisis management is a sensible step in setting up procedures. There will often be a point at which 'red flag warning' or 'amber alert' or 'action stations' or whatever term is preferred is more appropriate than a full plunge into crisis management. Such a procedure enables the team to go into readiness without completely disrupting the normal flow of business within an organisation and is particularly valuable where there are large numbers of false alarms or 'unclear situations' within a company's business, For example, many forms of transport business where unexplained delayed arrivals may trigger a 'red flag warning' but will frequently not develop into a crisis.

Preparation checklists

Full checklists, specifying in detail what each member of the crisis management team and each defined member of the support staff is expected to have
done and kept up to date in preparation for crisis, form a key part of the
manual and a basis for formal checking that the system is maintained in a
state of readiness. These checklists have the critical role of *defining* those
responsibilities which have already been allocated to specific individuals
and, in doing so, ensure that there are precise places where 'the buck stops'.
This is important because a state of preparedness for crisis will be extremely
difficult to maintain unless there are such clearly defined areas of responsibility.

   These preparatory check lists will not simply include simple mechanical
instructions such as 'check that all crisis room equipment is fully functional
at regular, not less than weekly, intervals', but will also cover more general
instructions such as 'Establish clear lines of communication with the following key publics/organisations . . .'.

   It will be these general instructions which provide both a preparation and
a training in the management of crisis by requiring an involvement from the
executive concerned which goes beyond purely mechanical responses.

Action checklists (management team and defined support team)

Under pressure of time and events nothing is easier to do than to omit some
important action which may not appear to be urgent. This can be very largely
guarded against by preparing full action checklists for all team and support
members in advance. These checklists are one part of the crisis manual
which should, and will, be referred to during the management of crises.
Duplicates of them should be held in the crisis room and in the desks of each
member of the support staff.

Action checklists (key functions)

In addition to action checklists for defined support staff and members of the
management team, similar lists need to be prepared for key functions which
will not act in a direct support role but which will be involved in the crisis and
exposed to its effects. The most obvious of these, and vitally important, is
the company switchboard which must have a precise set of instructions on
how to act when a crisis has been invoked, procedures for routeing incoming
calls and clear instructions on how to handle crisis related calls.

There may be other key functions which require similar lists. These will, again, depend largely on the nature of the business and on the type of risk. For example a retail chain will need to have such checklists for branch managers, in addition to instructions and training on crisis handling at store level.

Contact lists

Another part of the manual which will be referred to during the actual management of crisis, these lists need to be comprehensive and kept completely up to date. They should provide specific contact points within an organisation e.g. a senior police officer with whom dialogue has already been established on a particular concern, perhaps consumer terrorism. Substitute contacts should also be identified to be used in case of unavailability.

Contact lists will, typically, cover four separate groups.

- Internal contacts with key executives, advisers etc. within the corporate structure.
- External contacts with business partners and suppliers, e.g. PR consultants, company lawyers, suppliers, main distributors, shippers etc.
- Neutral, external contacts who are directly linked with the company, e.g. police, other public services, politicians with company links through industry or constituency association, possibly other companies in the same industry.
- External contacts with no direct connection with the company or particular interest in being supportive. These will include the media, special interest groups, Government departments etc. (Of course the degree to which these are potential allies at a time of crisis depends very much on the previous success of prior RRM activity.)

Although contacts will fall into one or other of these groups, it is not sensible to categorise them in this way in the contact listing except insofar as it aids speed of reference (e.g. internal as opposed to external). However some degree of awareness of potentially very different initial attitudes to contact by the company may be important at a time of making contact under crisis.

Just who is covered in these contact lists will depend very much on the company and the nature of its business. For example, some companies will regard contacts in Embassies overseas and foreign Embassies at home as being very important; while for other companies such contacts would be largely irrelevant.

Defining the scope of these contact lists and, in most cases, establishing a communication link, is part of the preparation for crisis. This should not be taken lightly. For no group is this more important than for the media and the way in which one manages contact with this particular, and very special, group will be of prime concern to the reputation risk manager. Knowing who to contact within the media is the first step.

Equipment checklist

Being physically equipped to manage a crisis is important and a full and clear listing of all equipment requirements, including switchboard systems to be invoked and procedures for obtaining priority in using standing equipment, fax, photocopying etc. needs to be set out in the crisis manual.

These are the essential elements of the crisis manual, although particular manuals will, almost certainly, carry additional material relating to particular circumstances. For example a major corporation will put crisis management programmes in place in its subsidiaries. These may well be very significant companies in their own right. Such manuals will need to carry a section on relating a crisis within the subsidiary to the overall corporate structure and the general corporate crisis management programme.

Smaller companies, aware of staff limitations and the consequent need to redeploy people outside their area of expertise in crises may feel the need to set out a whole series of very basic rules for carrying through some support functions. Where particular areas of potential crisis can be pinpointed, even anticipated (as discussed previously in risk assessment), very detailed instructions on handling a specific type of crisis may be included in the manual.

The purpose of the manual is to help prepare for and handle crises. Anything which enables the manual to do this more efficiently should be done, but this does not mean including everything which one can possibly think of. It cannot be over emphasised that the manual must be readily absorbable and easily used.

There are two additional items which are of considerable value both in preparing for and in handling crises, which may sometimes be included in the manual. On the basis that one does not want too much crammed between the covers one may feel that they are better omitted from the manual itself, but they certainly should not be omitted from the programme:

Prepared scenarios

A programme of risk assessment will have identified likely crisis areas, and, although not necessarily comprehensive, this means that scenarios can be prepared to reflect these areas of risk. The crisis programme can be tested against these scenarios and specific plans put in place to deal with likely eventualities (see discussion in Chapter 17). As a part of these scenarios, and on the basis of testing, it is also possible to develop decision trees as a management aid to dealing with the development of a real crisis which broadly reflects the scenarios. Such decision trees allow management to anticipate alternative developments and to be prepared to meet them even before they arise. In terms of regaining the initiative, this type of management aid can help enormously by saving time and placing you ahead of the developing situation. Such prepared scenarios and associated decision trees should be held in the crisis room for use as needed, even if not included in the crisis manual.

Prepared positions

In precisely the same way that scenarios and decision trees may be prepared on the basis of risk assessment so, too, a company's position may be pre-determined in relation to at least some crisis situations e.g. industrial action, legislative change. A pre-determined corporate positioning has the effect of allowing the crisis management team to start making decisions from a known base. This may also allow for prepared position papers and tactics which enable the initiative to be regained very rapidly. As with scenarios, such prepared positions should be held permanently ready in the crisis room.

The crisis manual will be a distillation of the crisis management programme and, as such, will, when studied analytically, pinpoint weaknesses in that programme. By centralising and formally setting down the key elements which go to make up the crisis management programme, it becomes far easier to identify omissions and short falls; and by testing the crisis management programme utilising the manual, these shortfalls can be picked up in practice as well as in theory. The manual effectively becomes more than a file of information, it becomes an intrinsic part of the programme itself. It is modified in the light of experience and changing circumstances and represents, at any one time, the state of a company's readiness for crisis.

SUMMARY

The crisis manual is the authoritative reference for crisis management. It must be:

- absorbable
- kept at the homes of the crisis team
- familiar.

Company culture will dictate the crisis manual format. However, in order to be effective it must cover:

- the context of crisis management within the company;
- corporate priorities at times of crisis;
- allocation of responsibilities (crisis management team, designated support staff and understudies);
- procedures for invoking crisis;
- full check list of responsibilities and equipment;
- prepared position statements.

The crisis manual will double as a training resource.

'AT THE COALFACE'
The Cambridge Vet School campaign

Lindy Beveridge

Large companies are not the only institutions which can find themselves facing a damaging and unexpected crisis. Early in 1989, Cambridge University learned to its surprise that the DES had decided to close both the Cambridge and Glasgow Veterinary Schools following publication of a report on veterinary education in the UK which had come up with this recommendation.

The decision was unexpected. The Cambridge Vet School was internationally renowned, attracting first class students and researchers and there is a shortage of vets in the UK. A decision to close it down would immediately create a crisis for Cambridge for a number of reasons. Students who had just been promised places would see them disappear before they could complete their four year courses. The Vet School had approved plans for two expensive new facilities, one of them a cancer treatment unit for which £1m had just been raised through a fundraising campaign; under the threat of closure, the School was likely to lose key staff; and the important contribution made by the School to biosciences and medical research carried out at Cambridge would be lost to the scientific community.

At that time, Cambridge University assigned a very small annual budget to PR activity and indeed its lack of attention to PR may have partly brought about the crisis. Most of the current budget had already been used up since the crisis came half way through the academic year. However, its academic departments have some discretionary funds for publicity materials and with the authorisation of their University administrator, also have access to a small additional discretionary budget. It was decided to pool these resources (about £6,000 in total) and to deploy the Vet School's full-time fundraiser plus a PR consultant, backed by free-of-charge use of the administrative resources of the University, to fight the decision and try to have it rescinded.

The timescale for the campaign was short – review of the recommendation and final decisions were due to be taken in early May, only nine weeks away. Moreover, during April the University Grants Council was due to go out of existence and be replaced by the University Funding Council, a new body consisting mainly of businessmen who knew little of university affairs.

The PR consultants advised on strategic and practical aspects of the campaign and worked closely with a University administrator who co-ordinated the academic input and liaised with the parliamentary lobbying campaign. Cambridge was careful to position its campaign so as to be seen to be fighting the cause of veterinary education in the UK rather than solely for the benefit of its own School since it is often seen as exceptionally privileged in terms of facilities for research in relation to other UK universities. In particular, since Glasgow had also decided to fight and had launched a vigorous campaign after hearing, via a leak, a couple of weeks ahead of Cambridge of its threatened status, care was taken not to undermine their campaign and animosity or competition with other UK vet schools was scrupulously avoided.

The first actions were for University administrators and academics to prepare a detailed and well written refutation of the case made for closure and for the Vet School's fundraiser to activate the friends and supporters of the Vet School to join the battle. A mailshot and direct appeal for help and signatures on a petition was sent out. Celebrities whose pets had been treated by the Vet School were contacted and asked for public support.

The PR consultancy set about writing up research topics of topical interest (e.g. work on dangerous dogs and BSE) and the history of the Vet School and these, plus the refutation document were assembled into a press pack and used to generate media coverage. Robert Rhodes James, the local MP, was briefed and assembled an all party supporters club in the Commons, all of whom received copies of the press pack. The membership of the about-to-be-born University Funding Council was researched and each member contacted and offered copies of the case against closure before they were due to start detailed consideration of the matter.

At the time, a major report on veterinary education was being prepared for the USA and Canada which took as its context the larger issues for veterinary education worldwide (scientific advance, the shift in types of animal ownership, conservation etc.). A copy of this report in draft was obtained via academic contacts and was available as background information for journalists or MPs on a discretionary basis. The object was to extend the debate beyond the competitive issues between UK vet schools and to encourage broad brush reviews of veterinary education in general.

Cambridge University called its first ever press conference in March. It was attended by a good turnout of journalists plus distinguished supporters of the Vet School. Speakers included the Vice-Chancellor, the Head of the

Vet School and professor Richard Perham, Head of the Department of Biochemistry and a highly respected life scientist. Their speeches addressed respectively the broad educational issues, the Cambridge case against closure and the contribution of the Cambridge Vet School to molecular biology and medical research on major diseases. A media campaign was directed to the national, regional and specialist press who by then had got their teeth into the Glasgow material. Good coverage was achieved including a leader in the *Daily Telegraph*. A letter to Robert Rhodes James from the Prime Minister, praising the excellence of the Cambridge Vet School, was successfully deployed to gain national and regional coverage. The petition signed by large numbers of supporters was taken to Downing Street by a couple of friendly celebrities, gaining TV and popular press coverage. Journalists were continually updated on the progress of the campaign.

The outcome of the campaign was that the decision was reversed in December 1989 and the foundation stone for the new cancer unit was laid in early 1990. Only one key member of staff defected during the campaign and the head of the Vet School was made a baronet in the following year. No adverse feedback was received from other vet schools who might have felt that Cambridge's success would divert resources from them. A sponsored victory cycle ride by Cambridge students round all the UK vet schools six months later was well received and generated positive goodwill.

Lindy Beveridge is Managing Director of Lindy Beveridge Public Relations Ltd, the Cambridge based public relations consultancy. She has particular expertise in handling high technology and scientific clients with their associated specialised areas of reputation risk.

16 EQUIPMENT FOR CRISIS MANAGEMENT

The physical equipment for managing crisis can be fairly straightforward, and ensuring that it is working and in place may be seen as relatively routine. This does not mean, however, that it should be regarded as unimportant or that it is not worthy of serious attention. Crisis equipment tends to be taken largely for granted until it fails to work properly, but when this happens the consequences may be far from trivial. As a rule there will be three areas of equipment provision which need to be considered:

1 Equipment and materials required by the crisis management team itself.
2 Equipment and materials required by the support team in handling direct aspects of the crisis.
3 Equipment and materials to be utilised in implementing decisions taken by the crisis management team.

Just as it is possible to ignore these physical needs to one's cost, so it is possible to make too much of an issue about physical equipment. There is a danger in doing this since it is all too easy to believe that one has prepared properly for crisis simply because one has been meticulous about ensuring that telephones, recording machines etc. are kept in working order. A sense of proportion and grasp of priorities is needed.

CRISIS ROOM CHECK LIST

A typical requirement for back up equipment and materials to be kept permanently in the crisis room would be:

- Direct line telephones equipped with recording facility.
- Television with access to relevant information services (Prestel etc.).
- Video recorder and supply of blank tapes.
- Where relevant, computer terminal with access to all centralised data.

- PC facilities including modem with dedicated line where appropriate.
- Radio with cassette recorder facility and blank tapes.
- Telephone extensions (filtered through a single checking point) for incoming calls.
- Copies of all relevant manuals (crisis manual, product recall manual, industrial relations procedures etc.).
- Individual copies of activity check lists for members of the crisis team.
- Prepared scenarios and decision trees.
- Stationery to include note pads, pens, pencils, telephone call log pads.
- General reference material – internal and external telephone directories, corporate organisation chart, etc.

Individual company needs may vary slightly. The physical means of ensuring that the crisis team remains in contact with all company information will depend on internal communications set ups, including computer networking. The type of general reference material which should be held in the crisis room may vary depending on an organisation's areas of operation and perceived exposure to crisis risk. It is possible to add a whole range of additional decision aids and mechanical supports but it is almost always a mistake to overdo the technology of crisis management. A point is rapidly reached where a plethora of decision aids actually hinders the process of managing a crisis, where speed and decisiveness is of the essence. All in all this listing of equipment and materials provides the basis for covering the needs of most crisis management teams.

SUPPORT TEAM EQUIPMENT

It is much less easy to provide a definitive listing of what will be needed by the support team directly involved in the handling of a crisis. In general support workers will need to be equipped with much the same facilities as the crisis management team itself. They will need dedicated telephone extensions, facilities for logging and recording calls, facilities to monitor and record TV and radio broadcasts, a filtering link into the crisis room which transmits critical information and the relevant action check lists for each member of the support team's particular function.

There may well be no need for there to be any additional equipment for the company switchboard – a key part of the crisis management support function, but there will be a need for procedures which allow for certain lines to be dedicated to crisis matters and for check lists to be available, to ensure that switchboard operators handle incoming crisis related calls in the pre-scribed manner. For some types of operation and for some types of crisis you will need a great deal more than this. Wherever there is likely to be public concern over a crisis, there must be a facility to deal with direct enquiries and to provide proper information to people who are involved. This is critically important whenever a crisis involves death or injury and there is a need to keep friends and relatives fully informed. (No one who saw TV pictures of unbriefed staff attempting to take down details from relatives on the back of scrap paper at the time of the *Herald of Free Enterprise* ferry disaster in the English Channel, could fail to be appalled at the apparent inability of the owners to react to a major disaster.)

The ability to provide such information will rely heavily on proper systems and equipment being in place to ensure that all calls are dealt with properly, that there are immediate information links established with the crisis area and emergency services, that there are dedicated telephone lines and an allocated number where concerned friends and relatives can make contact and that there is a system for ensuring that contact is made with friends and relatives as information becomes available. All this needs managing and requires formal systems to be in place which allow emerging information to be matched to particular areas of concern. Less dramatically than for such disaster scenarios, similar systems and facilities will need to be in place for dealing with distributor, retailer and public enquiries in cases of product contamination or product recall.

It is not within the scope of this book to deal with the mechanics of crisis management at the level of dealing with the specifics of an emergency. Indeed, it is probably beyond the scope of any book since each emergency is different and thus the precise requirements of each will also differ. There are, however, general rules which must be observed and not least of these is that a company involved in a crisis has a duty to minimise risk and distress resulting from this. Proper and full provision of information to those affected or concerned by the crisis is an important aspect of fulfilling this duty and will be a major factor in how the company is judged in relation to its handling of the crisis, with consequent effect on its long term reputation.

Perhaps the first person to recognise this was the American Ivy Lee, sometimes credited with being the inventor of the public relations business. He reversed the policy of US railway companies in the handling of disasters. At one time it had been normal railroad policy to surround any accident with a blanket of silence, which even included queries from relatives of passen-gers who might have been killed or maimed. Lee is credited with changing this policy and substituting a total openness of information.

It is interesting to note that Lee's reasons for making this change were because rumour and gossip were doing far more harm to the reputation of the railways than the truth could possibly do. His motivation was not so much one of corporate responsibility as one of reputation protection. In this more enlightened age corporate responsibility is taken far more seriously and one of the first consideration of a company will be to minimise public risk and distress. It is, indeed, fortunate that this is also precisely the right action to take to protect a company's reputation and that responsible behaviour coincides so precisely with enlightened self-interest.

The way in which people will expect to be able to obtain information from a company which is involved in a crisis has also changed considerably since the days of Ivy Lee. Today one has a right to expect to be able to obtain information fast and efficiently by telephone and through the virtually instantaneous media of TV and radio. In looking at the equipment and materials needed by the support team it is, therefore, important to ensure that there is a sufficient provision of communications and information storage equipment to enable the team to function efficiently when faced with the huge demand for urgent information which can result from certain types of crisis. Whether or not a company is exposed to risk of such a type of crisis is, of course, something which should have been established at the stage of reputation risk assessment within the RRM programme. Decisions should be taken at this stage on just what level of equipment may be required.

IMPLEMENTATION SUPPORT

It is pointless for the crisis management team to be taking decisions and working to regain the initiative in a crisis situation if the decisions which they are taking are not being put into immediate effect. This may seem a fairly obvious point but it should be remembered that during a crisis a company will normally still need to function in its normal operations. This continuity of activity may well be vital to the continued health of the company but it cannot be allowed to override the needs of the management of the crisis itself. This does not involve any special additional equipment or facilities but it does mean that there must be clear instructions that crisis management takes absolute priority in the use of all company facilities – fax, telex, electronic mail, photocopying, word processing, messenger services etc.

Appreciation of crisis will always be greater and faster at senior levels within a company. It is easy to forget that while the chief executive is taking decisions in an atmosphere of extreme pressure, central secretarial services may, at the start of a crisis, have little awareness that anything is happening. In recognition of this, it is worth having a formal procedure whereby the declaration of a 'crisis' automatically authorises priority over equipment and services rather than relying on an increasingly remote and junior chain of line management command to give priority to crisis activities on a case by case basis. In one particular case an overnight mailing providing information on a product recall was held up for four hours on an internal photocopying/ print plant because the print operatives gave priority to a routine mailing to company pensioners.

In general the rule is that the larger the organisation the greater the need to ensure procedures for giving action priority since command chains are longer and levels of awareness of central company issues are, in the short term, lower.

For the reputation risk manager the concern cannot be simply that the equipment, materials and systems are in place. It must also be to ensure that they are maintained in working condition and, in the case of checklists and other reference material, kept fully up to date. The whole of the crisis management apparatus needs to be kept in a state of readiness and needs to be tested and tried out on a regular basis, as discussed in Chapter 20. Such testing is insufficient for the equipment and a regular routine of weekly or, at worst, monthly checking should be instituted.

In practice, this maintaining of equipment and materials is an activity which will almost certainly be delegated and, subsequent to the initial decisions on what should be provided, does not require any great management skills. It is not, however, an activity which should be ignored or carried out with anything less than proper thoroughness.

17 INFORMATION AND DECISION AIDS

The question of information and decision aids has been touched on in the discussion of the crisis manual but it is worth taking a closer look at the form which these may usefully take.

The aim of such decision aids is twofold:

1 To highlight the main issues which are associated with particular types of crisis and ensure that none of these gets overlooked under the pressure of multiple decision making.
2 To provide the crisis management team with support guidance on decisions to be taken by indicating, in broad terms, the possible consequences of following particular courses of action.

CRISIS SCENARIOS

The form in which such aids are frequently produced is as prepared scenarios and decision trees, and their value is specific to RRM activity, particularly crisis preparation and crisis management. All of the other information material which we have looked at is either in the form of specific instructions (preparation and management check lists) or the gathering together of general information which will be needed for rapid reference at a time of crisis (contact lists and guideline notes).

Typically, prepared scenarios will postulate the development of specific forms of crisis and trace the way in which such crises will develop. In doing this a typical scenario will branch into a series of alternative developments dependent on what decisions are taken by the company in response to the situation. A straightforward example of this might be the decision whether or not to recall product in the face of some form of contamination threat – with further branching dependent on whether the threat turns out to be a hoax or a reality. Such scenarios must not be allowed to get out of hand or they rapidly enter the realms of creative fiction and are of little practical value. Nor can they be excessively detailed or they will contain such a wealth of information and choices that they are, again, of little practical use. Thus a scenario will not take the form of a detailed short story but will, rather, deal on a fairly broad brush basis. Postulated crises will be expressed in terms of 'Product contamination threat through consumer terrorism', or 'Plant accident resulting in fatalities and public danger' rather than 'Blackmail note found inserted in product packaging in Bolton supermarket', or 'Explosion of no 4 boiler at Leeds factory kills 3 workers and results in leakage of cyanide gas'.

Prepared scenarios should deal with those specific areas of possible crisis which have been identified as being genuine potential threats to a company and should concentrate on the main considerations which will arise from such threats should they develop into reality. They should deal with areas of concern and principles for action which have a general relevance to crises of a particular type. In this way the scenario will indicate particular actions which must be taken; choices which face the crisis management team and, through the 'branching' format mentioned above, possible consequences of those choices; key publics which need to be informed/persuaded; the corporate and external context within which the crisis should be viewed.

Growing directly out of the prepared scenarios is the production of management decision trees. These are, in effect, formalised versions of the branching character of a developing crisis. Because they are formalised they can be more detailed than the scenarios themselves and can include a degree of 'action reminders' associated with any decision which cannot be easily contained within a scenario. A decision tree of this nature will have much in common with the type of flow diagrams produced as standard management tools for project management but they are essentially different in that they involve exercise of judgement over events which develop outside one's control and the taking of decisions where the consequences can only be predicted with a limited degree of accuracy. They are not, therefore, a product of hard logic but rather of probabilities based on predictions and previous experience of similar situations.

CRISIS CHECK LISTS

For many companies this prepared scenario/decision tree approach may be considered overly elaborate and a straightforward check list of points for particular consideration by the crisis management team when dealing with particular types of crisis may be preferred. There is no gainsaying the fact that the amount of work involved in taking a scenario approach is much greater than that involved in producing 'things to consider' checklists. It is not clear how great the additional benefit obtained is from taking the more elaborate approach. However, it is clear that the scenario approach provides a much more thorough set of decision aids and that there is additional spin off benefit in training, testing and focusing attention.

My own preference is for a check list approach, mainly on the grounds that during a crisis everything needs to be kept as simple as possible and the very thoroughness of scenarios and decision trees can make them less valuable when a crisis develops in unexpected ways. (Taking the scenario/decision tree approach and developing it into a computer program might be a further way of dealing with this type of management decision aid, though one suspects that this would be of far more value as a training aid or specialist type of business game than as a practical management support tool.)

The form which these decision aids should take is not, however, a major issue in itself. What is important is that there should be decision aids which focus on particular types of crisis and provide guidance for the crisis management team on what are likely to be the main considerations in handling such situations. Irrespective of what form these crisis management decision aids take, the degree to which they will be of genuine help in a crisis will depend very largely on how accurately the original risk assessment work has been carried out as a part of the RRM programme. Quite obviously, the extent to which a prepared scenario mirrors the real events unfolding during a crisis is a measure of its value as a management aid during the crisis. Similarly, the value of decision trees or issue check lists is dependent upon their being related to the real decisions which have to be taken by the crisis management team.

Without a proper reputation risk assessment having taken place, it is unlikely in the extreme that it will be possible to produce scenarios or decision trees which have a great deal of value on the day of crisis. For some companies it may prove impossible to identify potential crises with a sufficient degree of accuracy to permit the development of detailed scenarios. For some companies the extent and sheer numbers of potential crisis scenarios may make the task of producing these dauntingly huge. In both these cases, however, it should still be possible to produce good, working check lists to cover all likely areas of risk. That there may need to be some fairly serious work done is not a sufficient reason for failing to carry out this type of work, which is of benefit both in dealing with crisis at the time and in preparing for crisis.

The value of producing such decision aids is not limited to the handling of crisis itself. They are a key training aid both for direct use in crisis 'rehearsals' and as a means of focusing attention on the type of issues and problems which will arise in a crisis and which will be largely common to all crisis situations. Despite their value, however, decision aids cannot be regarded as a substitute for the active use of judgement and management skill. Nor can they be expected to provide all the answers when one is actually facing a crisis.

All crises are different, and no crisis can be handled on a 'fly by wire' basis of prepared systems. The prime purposes of the type of decision aids discussed here will be to focus the mind on key issues to be considered; indicate the type of consequences which may result from certain types of decision; increase the extent to which events can be predicted in advance and, perhaps most importantly, set the crisis management team on a course which ensures that it manages a crisis and does not simply react to it.

'AT THE COALFACE'
Product Recalls

Peter Gavan

Product recalls are bad for business and should be avoided. They are expensive, time consuming for managers and workers alike, irritating and damaging to confidence in the company, trade, retailer and consumer. They are publicly embarrassing as well as costly. Handled well, recalls still don't *make* money, they lose cash from the bottom line. Recalls should be avoided where possible . . .

It is necessary to state all these very obvious negative consequences which follow a recall decision to put into context the work that myself and the Burson-Marsteller crisis management team in London and other countries across the world undertake. We attempt to try to find ways a company can avoid recall, or, if not avoid, then minimise its negative impact consistent with being a responsible company aware of its duty to all its audiences, particularly customers and consumers.

There is a grave danger that in writing an article like this about recall decisions and the communications consequences the reader might imagine that it is always obvious to management when a product problem determines a recall decision. It is not.

The Burson-Marsteller crisis management team has been involved in hundreds of discussions across the world when our clients have been faced with nasty problems. Some end up in high profile product withdrawal with international publicity; some end up in lower profile product withdrawals with national media or less attention being paid. Many, many more never reach the public domain because our clients, with our help and counsel, realise they do not need to shoot themselves in the foot, the head and elsewhere in the corporate body, by over-reacting.

A client might say to us, 'Obviously where there is any danger to health then you must always recall products. Let us examine this bland statement of perceived wisdom.

First of all, some products are 'dangerous' anyway so would never be sold against that criterion – and I do not mean cigarettes and cancer etc. Take some fizzy drinks in glass bottles. Occasionally some bottles and cartons can 'explode' due to glass weaknesses, bad handling, bad storage or a contents problem. Companies and consumers accept that these things can occasionally happen, maybe even resulting in a law suit if someone is accidentally injured. What does not happen just because of these incidents each year is that the product is withdrawn. Clearly companies have accepted a small element of risk to health in supplying their product. So do we as customers and consumers. Otherwise we would never drink alcohol, use glass bottles, eat mushrooms, eat yesterday's left overs etc., the list is endless.

So we have to step back from bland assertions that if there is 'any' risk to health we must alert the world and withdraw the product. There is always a role for judgement supported by counsel based on the wide experience held by crisis management teams like Burson-Marsteller.

Are there any *rules* which tell us immediately that a recall is necessary?

Obviously there are case studies – the most famous in the last decade being the Tylenol crisis which was held up at the time as the 'best practice' leader in crisis management terms. It involved the sudden deaths of seven people in the Chicago area, all of whom appeared to have been killed by cyanide in Tylenol capsules. Massive media coverage over the next several days led to understandable nationwide panic about Tylenol capsules and even Tylenol pills.

The Chairman of Johnson & Johnson took the decision to order a nationwide recall, even though the evidence pointed to a 'problem' localised in Chicago. That recall led experts to predict the end of Tylenol – the product was dead: several months later the company successfully relaunched Tylenol, even in capsules and was able within a remarkably short time to nearly regain its previous market share. The crisis cost an estimated $100m – but the product and company survived.

Contrast this with the more recent Perrier worldwide product recall. No deaths and no danger to health and no demand by governments for recall, not even the US Food and Drug Administration. But minor traces of benzene in the sparkling mineral water were sufficient – they really were tiny – to make Perrier decide to have a voluntary worldwide recall. Despite – or because of – its actions the company came under increasingly hostile pressure from the media in many countries, all demanding to know exactly what had happened.

Confusing and contradicting reports about the cause of the contamination and false reports that the Perrier source in Vergege, France, might be contaminated, threatened the product's usage of purity and the company's credibility and existence. Perrier turned to Burson-Marsteller to manage the communications on a global basis to rescue the company.

The trouble with these case studies is that they are not much use to a managing director if he or she has just been told some or all of the following late on a Friday before a bank holiday weekend:

> We have a problem.
>
> 'X' has been found in some of our product 'Y' – we think.
>
> We do not know yet how it got there – could be malicious.
>
> We do not know how wide spread it is.
>
> Some contaminated product may be in public domain – but we do not know how much stock or where it is precisely.
>
> Complaints have been received – but only usual number.
>
> A journalist has phoned saying he has heard we have a 'problem' – he does not appear to know any more than that – what do we say?

Hopefully this company would have a crisis management plan geared to coping with the sudden emergency. Maybe your product is connected with animal testing, with one or more separate accidents, maybe it is a natural extortion target because of its high profile due to TV advertising campaign . . .

So what advice can experienced product recall practitioners offer the company frantically searching for the **right thing to do?**

It boils down to judgements based on the best information available at the time. Where possible, we help clients prepare all the communications tools for recall at speed, working through the night, only the next day to be able to say on the basis of the latest information, we do not need to make a problem public or the possible problem has been contained at trade level or whatever.

However, sometimes a public recall is unavoidable. Then it may be possible to contain it within a distinct area, e.g. a town, county or region. It may also be possible to avoid appeals to the public across too broad an area. No one is going to thank companies for causing unnecessary alarm in a bid to create a 'caring, concerned' image through overkill.

There are three key questions that any company must be able to answer to avoid a communications disaster:

> What has happened?
> Who is to blame/What is at fault?
> What are you doing about it?

There are some basic ground rules for recall communications.

- Centralise control over communications so that consistent messages are given not just to media (trade, local, regional and national) but to all key audiences, e.g. employees, trade, supplies, regulatory.

- Draft press release, adverts, question and answer document in line with the consistent 'core' messages.

- Train spokespeople in advance – this is not the time to have training on the job.

- If necessary, set up a public information line. We use our sister company Telelab whose trained staff can handle hundreds of calls a day from trade, consumer and media after the number is issued publicly. This also allows a company's switchboard and staff the respite from the impact of being under siege.

- Another area often forgotten in recall handling is market research which should start as soon as there is public knowledge of the product's difficulty. This enables a company to track attitudes and adapt messages if necessary to meet concerns not immediately identified. It can also be useful in timing a product relaunch, although in the case of fast moving foods, these days the priority is usually just to get the product back on the shelves as quickly as possible.

So what should companies do to be in the best position to handle threats/problems that may/do result in product recalls? Prepare people and procedures is the simple answer but more difficult to actually do. As most companies do not go through regular recalls there is usually no built-up expertise to train and inform. At this stage it is sensible to consult those like B-M with the expertise to be able to check what is in place and recommend accordingly.

Then check again by simulation. However artificial simulation might seem compared to the reality, handled correctly, it can really test the communications procedures and skills of key individuals. The time to make mistakes is then, not during the period when the company is the goldfish bowl with everyone watching.

Role-playing actors and journalists, in the hands of experienced facilitators, can throw issues at a product recall team to illustrate the awful difficulties real life can throw at companies all too often. The aim is to build confidence, not destroy it, but unless your team sweats over a problem/issue the training experience is not of sufficient value.

In conclusion, product recall is survivable provided it is regarded in the same way as fighting fires. Fires sometimes happen and need to be put out quickly with the minimum of effort and damage. We also need to train and practice, not just how to avoid them, but also how to cope with the frightening experience of fire.

Peter Gavan joined Burson-Marsteller London in May 1989 and is Director, Issues and Crises Management. He works with clients facing difficult problems which have included extortion, product tampering and contamination, strikes, plant closures, hostages, environmental concerns and health issues.

18 MEDIA RELATIONS IN CRISIS

The subject of media relations is a complex one, covering a wealth of skills and techniques, and the subject of a large number of text books in its own right. No attempt can be made here to cover fully such an extensive subject, but nor can the importance of a subject which is critical to the successful management of reputation risk and of crisis be allowed to pass without some specific discussion; although, of course, the central role of successful media relations in defending against risk to reputation is implicit in virtually every chapter of this book.

In the long term the damage inflicted on a company or on a brand will depend on the attitudes which are held towards that company or brand by its key publics once a crisis is over. Reputations which have been built at huge expense will be damaged or even destroyed if perceptions of a company are altered for the worse as a result of crisis. The value of a brand can be virtually wiped out if public acceptance of that brand, and the way it is marketed as safe and ethical, is not achieved. For by far the greatest part of the key publics concerned, the information received and the interpretation to be put on this information will be obtained via the media. TV, radio, newspapers and magazines will provide the news, select supporting information, place their interpretation on the facts, and in general exert a massive influence on public perceptions.

For a company which has acted prudently and ethically and which reacts properly to the demands of a crisis the media are potential allies. For a company with something to hide, or even which fails to present its case sympathetically, the media are potential major enemies. Potential ally though the media may be, there is no commonality of interest with a company facing a crisis, or even a reputation threatening situation. The media's prime business is news and whether a story is good or bad for a company is of minimal consideration compared with how newsworthy it is.

Having said this it should also be said that the media are, by and large, reasonably responsible and, with some notable exceptions, are not in the business of distortion or misreporting simply for the sake of sensation. It is also true that, in general, the more serious the issue being reported, the more responsible will be the media's treatment of it. Most of the time that people complain about having been misrepresented in the press or on the broadcast media, they have not been misrepresented at all but have simply said or done something which, on mature reflection, they wish they had not. Or they have simply failed to put over their views or their position in a way which can be properly understood.

The media may prove to be an extremely valuable help in the actual management of crisis. They provide the channels for disseminating information to the public extensively and rapidly, whether this information be the telephone number of the crisis hot line, reassurance about unfounded rumours or straight instructions about sensible action to take (such as returning unused product which may have been tampered with to the point of purchase). By and large this aspect of media relations is relatively straightforward, taken by itself. But it cannot be taken by itself. No journalist, no matter what medium they work in, is going to want to act simply as a bulletin board but will want to gain maximum news coverage from any story and to be in a position to place this in context with background information and comment. It is not so much the media's role as information provider but rather its role as an opinion former which will be of particular concern to the RRM manager.

In a crisis situation, it will be media coverage which has largely contributed to the fact that a company's reputation is endangered. Indeed, it may well be media coverage which has turned a problem into a crisis. It is also the media which holds the key to salvaging that reputation. If a company is to ensure that public perceptions of it are as positive as possible, then it will need to manage its relationships with the media with considerable skill and a degree of openness. These are people whom one wants on one's side and secrecy is no way to achieve this. If you have a job to do and someone makes it easier for you to do it, then you will tend to offer help in return. By the same token if someone is obstructive and unhelpful then you are likely to be similarly unhelpful in return. Journalists have a job to do and will normally react in just the same way as anyone else to help and to hindrance.

While it is not possible to set out a total strategy for media relations here, it is possible to set out a few of the basic rules and broad principles which should normally be adopted in handling the media during a crisis. Like any rules they are there to be broken and there may be occasions when a totally different approach is indicated. But if one is to depart from the basic principles then one must have a very good reason for doing so and be aware of the possible consequences.

SOME BASIC RULES

• **Decide on the media relations strategy from the start but be prepared to modify tactics.** The fact that one is dealing with a crisis situation should not be a reason to handle everything on an unplanned, *ad hoc* basis. This applies to media relations as to any other aspect of crisis management. Time taken at the start to determine media relations strategy, key messages which need to be disseminated and the most effective ways of doing this will always prove to be time well spent. The principle of seizing the initiative when managing crisis should not be confused with unplanned and unconsidered action.

Although strategy should be determined early, one must recognise that tactics will have to be flexible. Circumstances change rapidly in a developing crisis and no media relations plan can afford to be so rigid that it cannot be modified to meet such changes.

• **Co-operate with the media to the fullest extent possible which is consistent with protecting the company's interests**. While co-operation with the media is strongly advocated, the *caveat* of consistency with company interests is an important one. The media do not have the same priorities or interests as a company in crisis and this should never be forgotten.

• **Be as even-handed as possible in dealing with the media.** There is absolutely no percentage in playing clever games with the media when facing a crisis which is of general public interest. It must be the conscious aim of media relations activity to let everyone have the same information at the same time. Of course there will be existing press contacts which may be more receptive to receiving additional information but this should not be offered on an exclusive basis. There will be decisions to be taken about agreeing to TV and radio interviews and not everyone will be able to be accommodated, but the yardsticks on which decisions are made should be applied similarly to all requests for interview.

• **Take the initiative as rapidly as possible.** As early in a crisis as possible, one wishes to move to the position of issuing information and explanation on one's own initiative rather than simply reacting to media requests. By doing this one begins to exercise a measure of control over content, timing and emphasis of coverage, and at the same time one presents the company as being both open and co-operative in its dealing with the crisis.

● **Maintain rigid control over what is said or given to the media.** It is vital to control what is said to the media, to ensure that there are no 'off the cuff' comments and that nobody, other than authorised spokespersons, have any discussion with the media. In practice this means that the team handling incoming media calls must stick rigidly to the text of approved press releases and prepared statements. The only people who will hold any kind of briefing discussions with the media are the company spokesperson (usually the crisis management team chairperson) and the RRM manager. No other member of the company, however senior, may comment on or discuss any aspect of the crisis with any external party without prior approval.

● **Do not make promises you cannot keep.** There are few things more irritating to a journalist who is working towards deadlines than to be promised information or an interview which is not then forthcoming. A promise to 'ring back within half an hour' or to 'fax over some background information' to 'issue a press statement at 3 o'clock' or whatever must be honoured.

● **Stick to hard information and do not waffle or bluster.** This is not merely good advice for handling TV and radio interviews but should apply to all aspects of media relations, from issuing press statements through to conducting a full press conference. It is a sound principle of all media relations work, whether connected with managing reputation risks or not, but is particularly timely advice to heed during crisis management.

● **Do not suspend normal good practice rules of media relations simply because you are in crisis mode.** It is, if anything, more important to observe the simple basics of good practice of media relations during a crisis than at any other time. Press statements should be issued with an awareness of deadlines, should be factual and contain the main story at the beginning, should always carry a contact name and telephone number, should be typed double-spaced and with wide margins, should be on only one side of the paper. Interviews, with both broadcast and printed media, should be prepared for and comment confined to facts. Press conferences should have genuine news content and should justify the conference format for information dissemination. These and all the other myriad rules which are observed in any competent media relations operation should be adhered to during crisis management. They help the media to do their job and they protect the company from allowing media contact to move out of control.

● **Disseminate information fast.** In a crisis one will wish to get one's message across to as many people as possible as quickly as possible. As soon, that is, as one is clear what that message needs to be. There will often be a need to delay any public comment until one has assessed a situation and is sure of the facts, but as soon as one has something which one wishes to say one wishes to get it out fast. Maximum use should therefore be made of all methods for getting a story out widely and quickly utilising news agency wire services, electronic mail link ups, fax etc.

Preparation for the rapid, extensive distribution of media information will have been a part of the RRM programme and, come the day, full use should be made of this, essentially mechanical but important preparation.

● **Do not be flustered into panic action.** This is an obvious point and very easily set down as a rule. In a real crisis, it is a rule which can be very difficult to follow. All of the encouragement to seize the initiative in a crisis, all of the emphasis on time being vital, all of the pressure which will be felt from the media demanding a story and seeking a unique angle, even the normal PR instinct to help the media as far as possible, will conspire together to stampede one into precipitous or ill-considered action.

There is a fine line between co-operating with the media and being manipulated by the media. This line gets crossed the moment that one allows media pressure to outweigh other considerations in handling the information interface between the company and the outside world.

None of these rules is particularly clever or particularly obscure and, to the PR professional, they will have the ring of the blindingly obvious. In fact, it is quite astonishing how often they are totally ignored by companies engaged in managing a crisis, even when media relations activity is in the hands of experienced and capable PR operatives where they lack training or experience of crisis management. They are rules which apply just as much to RRM as to the management of the developed crisis and they are based on the simple principle that the best way to deal with the media is through co-operation, coupled with the recognition that co-operation has its limits and that an alliance between a company and the media is an alliance of convenience and does not imply an identity of interests.

DO NOT COUNT ON THE MEDIA

The final, and the most important, rule of media relations during any form of

RRM, including crisis management, is not to count on the media as the sole channel for one's information strategy. For all the reasons discussed above, the media cannot be controlled. They can be helped, persuaded, managed and befriended but at the end of the day, they are their own creatures. The media is, at best, a flawed vehicle for disseminating information in the way in which a company wishes it to be presented. It has the benefits of reaching huge audiences and, where what it has to say is positive, of providing a third party endorsement to company information. It has the disadvantages of being generalist in its approach and of presenting information in the way it chooses under the influence of what makes a good news story. It is not the means by which one chooses to communicate with one's key publics if any alternative is available.

Wherever messages can be sent to key publics through direct communication this should be done. Fax, telephone, telex, and mail should all be used to the fullest extent to ensure that direct transmission of the information which one wishes to provide is achieved, without passing through the filter of media editing and interpretation. The key publics which need to be addressed, and which will represent a company's most important external relationships, will have been identified as part of the RRM programme. If they have not been identified in advance then this will be an early priority as part of the crisis management activity. Reliance on the media to provide information to these key publics is foolhardy. Failure to make full use of any opportunity of direct communication with these key publics is a serious omission.

19 RESEARCH AND FEEDBACK

Research is usually regarded as a comparatively long term activity and, although its role is fairly obvious in RRM both for identifying reputation risk areas and for monitoring how effectively these are being managed, is often wrongly thought to have no part to play in full scale crisis management. However, research can play a central role in determining tactics during the management of crisis, just as it will have played its part in determining strategy during pre-crisis planning.

The use of research to obtain feedback on attitudes and perceptions during a crisis will achieve two main objectives:

- It will enable the crisis team to identify the issues which are of real concern to its key publics and towards which it should direct its information strategy.
- It will enable the crisis team to monitor changes in these attitudes and the development of any fresh problem areas as the crisis develops and is managed.

In the final analysis it will be the successful communication of the right messages to key publics, i.e. those messages which address the questions and concerns of those publics, which will provide effective management of perceptions and attitudes in a crisis. Put rather less pompously this comes down to telling people what they want to know and answering whatever is worrying them.

Without some form of research which provides feedback from outside the company, one does not really know what these attitudes are. Certainly, the media will reflect what they believe to be of importance and, as we have discussed, may actually create areas of concern. It is by no means clear, however, that media interest will provide an accurate reflection of public interests. For example public concern in the case of a product recall will probably be about what, if any, risks there are in buying the product once it is reoffered for sale. Media interest will tend to continue to be focused on the issues surrounding how and why the original recall took place.

It is clear that where an organisation does not identify and address the real concerns of its key publics then it has little hope of effectively managing information flow during a crisis. Identifying real concerns, without the input of some form of attitudinal research, will depend on guesswork. However well informed such guesswork is, it cannot be as good as hard, attitudinal data. In the hot house atmosphere of crisis management it is very easy to lose the sense of perspective which is essential for even passably good guessing.

During crisis it is not usually possible to conduct detailed, in depth surveys. It is possible, however to conduct telephone surveys where the crisis is a major one and effects the general public. It is also possible to conduct 'straw poll' research amongst members of key publics where a crisis impacts on specific specialised publics e.g. the City, retail outlets etc.

A good example of the importance of identifying where the real problem lies is provided by the 'Listeria Hysteria' crisis of confidence in soft cheeses which occurred in the UK and which has been referred to previously in a different context. In this instance the level of public concern was far lower than was indicated by the overreaction of the press, as was the public understanding of the very small sector of the populace which might be placed at risk. Moreover, public concern passed very quickly, possibly due to the fact that so many separate food scares had been plastered over the press within a very short period.

The real problem which faced soft cheese producers, and particularly French producers, was that the retail trade was far more worried than the public and withdrew product from sale in retail stores. The communications need was primarily one of reassuring the retail trade and getting soft cheeses back on display. It was not so much a matter of persuading the public to buy the product as making sure that they had the opportunity to buy. The longer the product remained off the shelves, the more sales would be lost and, just as important, the buying habit of favouring soft French cheeses which had been established at considerable cost in promotional expenditure would be lost among recently converted cheese eaters.

Without feedback from research, it would have been difficult to identify where the real problem lay or to develop the successful strategy of making the retail trade the primary short term target whilst addressing residual public concern as a secondary, longer term objective. Certainly this strategy could not have been developed on the basis of media attitudes, and probably not on the basis of guesswork alone.

It is a basic requirement of all communications activity that there should be a two way flow of information and that what one wishes to communicate should be presented in terms which are accessible to one's audience and relevant to one's audience's interests. A crisis room during an operation is not a good place to judge audience interest or attitude. If a full RRM programme has been in operation there will be an awareness of probable attitudes and an identification of where a company's real reputation problems lie in advance of any crisis developing, but this awareness will be approximate and will change. Reliance on media coverage to reflect what the public really believes is not satisfactory. On the contrary, it can be positively misleading. Reactions and attitudes need to be researched objectively and need to concentrate on the effects of the crisis on the identified key publics, not on commentators or peripheral interests.

The process of monitoring reaction needs to be formalised and this needs to be done on a continuous basis since attitudes can shift over short periods during crisis – partly in reaction to information received and partly in reaction to the way in which this information is interpreted and presented by the media. This monitoring of attitudes will be one responsibility of the reputation risk manager, and it will be his or her responsibility to ensure that it is used in forming information strategies in relation to the crisis. Whether this is done by using outside experts or by an in-house team is not important, but it is important that objective criteria should be used and that, in tracking attitude changes, there is a consistency of approach.

20 TESTING AND TRAINING FOR CRISIS

It has been a continuing theme throughout our discussion of RRM that prevention is better than cure and that the avoided crisis is always to be preferred to the managed crisis, no matter how well managed. Unfortunately it is not always a matter of choice. Certainly companies find themselves facing crises which could have been avoided. Certainly there have been many crises which could have been defused before they developed into full crisis proportions. However there will always be crises which can neither be avoided nor defused. The unavoided crisis is a fact of business life.

At the heart of everything which has been said about crisis management during the last few chapters has been the notion of preparation. Although any particular crisis will almost certainly be unexpected in terms of its specific occurrence, the fact that there is a need to handle a crisis should not, in itself, be a surprise. 'Why this issue?', 'Why today of all days?' may be legitimate reactions in the face of crisis. 'What on earth should I do?' is not.

Preparation is fine so long as it is the right preparation and as long as it remains relevant. These are two separate considerations and should be recognised as such. Making sure that one has got an effective crisis management capability in place is one thing and ensuring that that capability is maintained in a state of readiness is another. They are treated here together because the practical steps which one takes to achieve the one should also have the effect of achieving the other. Even so it is worth making the point that testing procedures and training exercises should always be designed in the awareness that there is a twin goal to be achieved. It is no use maintaining the whole elaborate paraphernalia of crisis management capability in a state of readiness if it has not been tried to see if it actually works. By the same token it is no use establishing an effective, planned and tested structure for crisis management if that structure is going to be allowed to deteriorate into ineffectiveness.

We have already discussed the need to keep all relevant information up to date on a running basis, ranging all the way back to reassessing reputation risk areas regularly through to updating contact names and telephone numbers in the crisis manual. The need to keep a continuing check on equipment and materials has also been covered. The crisis management system itself and the people who make up the crisis management team and its support are in no less need of being equipped to carry out the job and maintained at a level of readiness to do so when the need occurs.

TESTING OVERALL CAPABILITY

It should not be necessary to test a corporation's crisis capability in total with any great level of frequency. Indeed it may be necessary to run such a full scale trial only once in order to test that the system as set up is capable of operating in crisis. Subsequent to this it may be enough to put into place the lessons learned from such a test and to check on separate aspects of the system on a fairly regular basis, without becoming involved in the level of disruption which a full scale test is likely to involve. There is no better, indeed no viable, way of testing the effectiveness and readiness of total crisis management capability other than by running a mock crisis and checking how systems and people perform in crisis conditions. Such tests must clearly be as realistic as possible and, on occasion, it may be possible to run an exercise without the personnel involved being aware that they are not involved in the real thing. Generally, however, it will not be possible to run a test without those involved being aware that it is an exercise.

A word of warning about running a totally realistic exercise is probably in order. If one attempts to do this then one must make sure that one has provided absolute controls to ensure that it does not get out of hand and even develop into a crisis of its own. Consider, for instance, the effects of running a phony product contamination exercise where the effect is to start rumour running through the press and the retail trade; or a chief executive held to ransom exercise where the false scenario gets back to the City as if true.

In general, then, it will be necessary for participants to know that what they are involved in is an exercise. This does not, however, mean that such an exercise cannot be made an extremely testing experience for the individuals involved, nor that it cannot be structured in such a way that systems are put fully to the test. Realism is the key and the way that this is best achieved is through thorough planning which takes into account a set of alternative developments of the crisis.

An effective method of doing this is to take one of the identified reputation risk areas for a company and develop the outline scenario prepared for this into a higher degree of detail. Thus as the crisis management team takes, or fails to take, critical decisions, the next stage of the developing crisis can be fed back to them. In this way the crisis is played out even faster than in real time and a level of pressure is built up which mirrors the type of pressure felt in the real event, even though participants are aware that they are involved in an exercise.

It is not just the crisis management team which is under test in such an exercise, however, but the whole of the support team and the systems which have been instituted. The structure of the test should, therefore, allow for testing of these aspects of crisis management also. Thus, there should be an element of incoming telephone calls to test switchboard alertness and procedures; implementation of crisis management team decisions must be taken through to a point at which it is clear that full implementation can take place e.g. identifying locations of an entire batch of product; preparing a full press statement together with distribution list and method for disseminations; setting up and manning a relatives' information service and hot line facility, etc.

If it is practicable, the exact timing of the exercise should not be revealed in advance. It will be necessary to let people know that such an exercise will be taking place and to give some indication of when this will happen. This indication of timing should, however, be as general as possible if one wishes to see how effectively the company can move into crisis mode at short notice. Within the constraints imposed by the fact that this is only an exercise and the company has got a day-to-day business to run, it should not be possible for participants to prepare too much in advance. A further factor of the unexpected can also be provided by ensuring that at least one 'first team player' is unavailable at the start of the exercise, forcing the use of substitutes for at least part of the time. While participants will know that a crisis management exercise is scheduled to take place, they should not know the form which the exercise will take nor the area of reputation risk which will be the focus of the exercise.

It will almost certainly be necessary to involve some expert outside help in running a testing exercise on total crisis management capability for a number of reasons:

● Outside consultants will have previous experience of developing crisis scenarios and introducing fresh elements as the exercise develops in a manner which will enable systems and personnel to be tested in ways which are not immediately predictable. It is very difficult for someone who has been responsible for setting up a crisis management system to identify weaknesses within it.

- Outside consultants will have the resources to 'role play' the necessary inputs into the crisis, (incoming media queries, Government departments, legal threats, distraught relatives etc.) and to do so in a way which is far more 'real' to participants than can be achieved by colleagues within the company.
- Thanks to their relative objectivity, outside consultants are in a strong position to assess company performance and pinpoint areas which may be usefully worked on or modified.
- The range of experience of outside consultants is likely to be much wider than that available within the company in terms of crisis management. They will be able to look at the crisis management programme in action against this background of comparison.

The question of assessment of performance is an important one. The results of running a full testing exercise must be carefully analysed and steps taken to correct any areas where either people or systems have failed to perform properly. If this is not done then the benefits of the exercise will be largely lost. The point is to identify what might go wrong in handling a crisis if and when one occurs and to avoid having to discover this the hard way during a real crisis.

There is a near infinite range of things which may turn out to need adjustment or change as a result of running a full capability check. The following list of areas to look out for cannot even begin to be a comprehensive one. It does, however, indicate some of the commonest areas for concern of which I have become aware through involvement in crisis management and crisis management training activity:

- Tendency for the crisis management team to remain in a reactive mode and not take decisions which regain the initiative.
- Tendency for the crisis management team to take an overly defensive and company protective position with eventually very negative results for the company. (Very difficult to spot in a simulation but obvious enough in a number of real crises where management's initial reaction of denial and minimising rebounds e.g. Exxon oil spill in Alaska.)
- Failure of support team to provide sufficient up-dated information to the crisis management team – and similarly management team's failure to take sufficient external advice.
- Failure of support team to filter out information to the management team

resulting in a 'white noise' effect and interference with management ability to focus on key issues.

- Systems failures of all sorts, ranging from switchboard procedures not being implemented through to key contacts not being informed and, where necessary, consulted.
- Inability to retrieve vital information from normal corporate sources under pressure e.g. location of product identified as having been contaminated, full passenger information for vehicle/plane/ship involved in a disaster etc.
- Failure to anticipate reaction from other involved parties. (Again difficult to spot in a training exercise but obvious enough in cases such as different divisions of a multinational issuing conflicting statements, or an industry group's efforts to handle a generic product problem being directly undermined by Government department activity.)
- Failure to identify crisis conditions and invoke crisis management procedures quickly enough.
- Failure of crisis team, management and support, to have familiarised themselves with procedures and their roles in advance.
- Inadequate or unhelpful support information available to the crisis management team in the crisis room – scenarios, decision trees, reference information, check lists, contact lists etc.
- Equipment failure or malfunction (which may include nobody knowing how to use it and no handbook available).

One often finds that running the exercise has the effect of putting right a number of weaknesses, particularly where these relate to the performance of individuals. As a training medium in crisis handling there is nothing to beat 'hands on' experience of the real thing, and a well run mock crisis exercise of the type described is the next best thing.

FUNCTION TESTING

Once the total crisis handling capability has been tested, results should be analysed, necessary adjustments made to procedures and, where appropriate, additional training provided for individuals. It should not be necessary to repeat such full scale testing except at very long intervals where one suspects that the system has deteriorated through neglect or if significant changes have occurred within the company or its business environment to an extent which demands similarly significant changes in its approach to crisis handling. Running a full scale exercise is, inevitably, both time consuming and disruptive. It is unnecessary where the individual functions which go to make up the total capability can be tested separately and far less dramatically on a regular basis.

This individual testing is worth doing and achieves a number of objectives:

- It provides a formal check that specific parts of the system continue to function properly.
- It enables new personnel, inevitable with recruitment, promotion etc, to be integrated into their roles within the crisis team.
- It acts as a continuing reminder to people with roles to play at a time of crisis that this is a real responsibility and in doing so maintains a level of crisis awareness.
- It helps identify any special training needs which exist and allows these to be dealt with on an individual basis.

This type of update checking will vary depending on which aspect of the system is under test. Often it may be sufficient to simply run through the procedures involved with the people concerned. Sometimes it is helpful to run through mini-exercises or work shop sessions. For crisis management team personnel, testing may take the form of simplified management games where the substitutes compete against the first team in handling an imaginary crisis.

Just how one approaches this 'topping up' process is very much a matter of judgement and, to an extent, style. In some companies members of the support team act out management team roles in a simulated crisis with the aim of gaining a greater appreciation of the importance of their roles by understanding what is happening in the 'command post'. Other companies include simulated crisis management as a regular part of management training and include it in residential 'think tank' weekends. The individual approaches will vary depending on company culture and structure but the broad objectives remain the same i.e. to maintain an awareness and capability to handle crisis. Without such a process of topping up, crisis handling capability atrophies and the effort put into creating systems in the first place is largely wasted.

INDIVIDUAL TRAINING

On the job training for crisis management through the types of activity described above will prove sufficient to meet most company needs. There will, however, be some areas of specific skills which will need developing and which may be vital during a crisis – particularly in relation to protecting the company's reputation at such a time through influencing the way in which its attitudes and actions are perceived. These particular skills are not usually specific to crisis management but it is then that they come most dramatically into their own.

Media training

During a crisis there needs to be a 'face' to a company in the form of a spokesperson – the role normally taken on board by the chairman of the crisis management team. Perceptions of a company's performance and attitudes at a time of major crisis in the public arena will be largely formed by the impressions created by the company spokesperson. He or she will need to be prepared to give TV, radio and press interviews, often in the face of hostile questioning. This is not something which can be done without experience and training and such training, readily available from a number of specialist companies, should be provided to all senior personnel who may find themselves needing to act as corporate spokespersons at short notice.

The point that perceptions are only contingently related to reality has been made many times previously and nowhere is this more true than in the TV or radio interview where a poor performance counts for more than the strength of argument. Press interviews carry equally dangerous, but rather different, pitfalls.

Telephone answering

At a time of crisis members of the support team are likely to be placed in the position of dealing with telephone queries of a type and intensity to which they will not normally be accustomed. The crisis manual check lists will provide guidance for this and, in some circumstances this may be sufficient, although a degree of practice in handling particularly difficult types of call is still recommended. Where there is likely to be a special requirement, however, e.g. the information service provided in the wake of a transport disaster, special training can, and should, be given.

Information distribution

Most PR departments will believe that they are more than competent to handle distribution of information to the media, but when it comes to crisis management this may well not be true. The amount of experience that the average 'in-house' PR department has with dealing with news coverage at TV, radio, national and major provincial press level is frequently very limited. Training may well be necessary to ensure familiarity with this type of media relations – a far cry from trade press, specialist correspondents, feature writers or even routine news coverage.

There may well be other types of specific training for individuals which are identified as useful for particular companies over and above these three areas. In general, however, people acting in a crisis will be drawing on the skills and knowledge which they employ every day in their jobs within an organisation. The difference in crisis is that there is a complete change of pace, pressure and priorities. It is not, therefore, that new skills are required, rather that existing skills need to be used differently and with an adjusted attitude of mind.

It is no accident that the three areas of special skills identified as calling for individual training are all related to the company's information interface with external publics. It is this interface which determines perceptions of the company and, thus, much of the long term effect of the crisis on its business. It is also managing this information interface which will call on skills which, generally speaking, will not be in day-to-day use within the company.

'AT THE COALFACE'
Tests, trials and tribulations

William Comery

INTRODUCTION

Creating crisis management programmes is an example of a situation where you are left hoping that what you have created is never put to the real test, perfect as you know it is. But testing the protection should and can be part of any crisis management programme, and these tests come in one of two forms. Open testing exercises, where participants know that the operation is only an exercise, have their place in checking everything except for one vital ingredient – the people involved. To discover how this most central component will operate under the pressures that only a major incident can produce one has to test blind, when, to the participants, there will be none of the reassurance that mistakes will have no consequences. In circumstances like these, pressures build up and, when it is finally revealed that all was only a test – even if a vital one, the release of that pressure may well be directed at those who organised the event. This piece describes just such an exercise which was organised for a client recently.

The client is an international FMCG company, manufacturing and selling in most major geographic markets. Like any sensible company of any size it has its procedure manuals to cover emergencies and it has its crisis management procedures. To test the effectiveness of the latter we picked one of its markets – the Middle East – and two highly sensitive issues for that market – pornography and alcohol – and added a third – smuggling – of more than passing interest to any authorities anywhere. We made the consequences of failure to contain the crisis great for the worldwide parent company as well as for the unit that was our immediate client/guinea pig. Careful planning was essential before putting this test into action.

LIMITATIONS

The first check list comprised those factors that set the limits to what we could do and test. This included:

- An understanding of the objectives – their scope and their limits.
- The minimum of client staff concerned who had to know that it was all only an exercise – the ideal is zero, we managed three.
- A scenario and methodology that would ensure containment within the unit being tested. The last thing that one wants of a crisis practice is that it creates a crisis proper.
- Credible outsiders to unfold the mounting crisis. For our plan we needed several journalists, government representatives and on the ground client representatives. We employed a company specialising in such role-play – luckily there are a lot of 'resting' actors around nowadays – who were instructed not to take return calls.
- Reserve, fall back scenarios to cover all likely courses of action taken by the participants.
- A way of maximising benefit in the case that the exercise is rumbled.

Not withstanding the requirement to test as much as possible of the crisis programme, a time had to be chosen that would minimise the disruption to normal business – the client should not lose out avoidably in running the exercise. We chose a Friday – conveniently equivalent to a weekend for the Arabian market with which we were operating. A concisely defined timespan was necessary, we chose to make the affair last for a day so that participating staff would not go home worrying about the issues at a time when they were unable to take any ameliorating action.

OBJECTIVES

As well as wanting to test the effectiveness of the existing crisis programme, we also wanted to test the awareness of the need to use the programme and whether it was invoked at the appropriate time. We wondered whether there would be any institutionalised unwillingness to start so serious a train of events or contact very senior people with such unpleasant news – to behaving like an ostrich in the face of serious unwelcome events is a common reaction.

We obviously wanted to test the performance of staff under this unique kind of stress and learn whether we had the right people in the right positions. Several already existing internal systems were important subsidiary parts of the crisis programme. How would product tracing/recall and switchboard routines (the immediate face that any company presents to its publics) stand up? Finally, the process of carrying out the exercise would both raise the awareness of the importance of crisis management and also help train the staff. A fictitious scenario and a strict timetable were planned to provide a testing and controlled operation.

SCENARIO

General

Client shipment containers packed in the UK were found by customs in Kuwait and Saudi Arabia to have been used to smuggle in alcohol and pornography. Client complicity would be suspected in such circumstances.

This fiction was created and developed by a series of telephone calls from several press and government sources. The matter escalated erratically, with inconsistencies and irrelevancies thrown in, as happens in real life.

Detailed

The possibility that client container/case(s) have been used to smuggle alcohol and pornography into a Gulf State, probably Saudi Arabia but possibly Kuwait.

Warehouseman with access to our containers, and ability to open them, has admitted in a newspaper interview that he has been responsible for such smuggling. Customs connivance seems certain in this.

The interview results from a tip off that a major consignment was sent by him to the Middle East in the last month.

There is no certainty that client was involved but 'food' was stated in the interview, therefore there is a strong likelihood that a client consignment was involved.

The tip off was from journalist J., publisher of the Middle East . . . The story was from one of his Arabic speaking freelances. There is no immediate police involvement but the possibility exists of follow up procedures in the UK. There is a near certainty of police involvement in Saudi/Kuwait. The journalist involved also 'strings' for the Gulf . . . . The story has been killed at the UK end at present for want of hard evidence and a general unsuitability of the story for ME . . . .

We can assume early police searches in Saudi/Kuwait; we should assume a likely backlash from press coverage; we should assume that if drink or pornography is discovered in our packaging then a total ban on imports is likely in the target country and possibly throughout the Gulf States.

From this starting point the scenario will unroll during the day. The timetable will be adhered to as far as possible, but it must be accepted that events may distort the pattern.

Timetable

9.00 am	Journalist J telephones client, asks for managing director (MD), speaks to ? and outlines first stage of scenario.
9.20 am	Consultancy rings client, speaks to senior executive and reinforces story.
9.45 am	Consultancy rings client with further detail from journalist J.
10.00 am	Reputation risk manager (RRM) arrives (invokes crisis programme if necessary), summons consultant.
10.00 am onwards	MD contactable.
10.30 am	MD available in office at earliest.
11.15 am	Journalist J telephones – call to Incident Room over loudspeakers. Vessels, port and product involved identified. Confirms inevitability of information being provided to Gulf News Agency and Saudi Authorities. Confirms possible UK police involvement.
12.00 noon	RRM to contact client manager in locality (if available) and explain 'only an exercise – no action, no panic'.
12.30 pm	Telephone call from 'Gulf News Agency' asking for comment and advice.
1.05 pm	Telephone call from 'Saudi Embassy' requesting clarification.
1.25 pm	Telephone call from 'Kuwait Embassy' requesting clarification.
2.00 pm ish	Dubai agent telephones – urgent message, rumours circulating in Ministry of Health.
3.00 pm – 4.00 pm	Five Pan Arab media telephone calls.
4.00 pm	Further call from 'Saudi Embassy' – 'very serious view being taken'.
4.15 pm	Repeat call from 'Gulf News Agency'. Request one to one interview with 'Managing Director'.

| 5.15 pm | Person to person call 'Prince N' to RRM: Videos and Alcohol traced to Saudi contact, 'Mr S', interviewed by Saudi Guards/ Customs and warrant for detention of local manager – Police/ Customs at warehouse – journalists aware throughout Saudi. |
| 5.45 pm | Cancel exercise. |

STRENGTHS AND WEAKNESSES ANALYSIS

The advantage that outweighed all other advantages and all disadvantages was that staff were put under the stress that they would have to face in reality. As in reality, there could be no preparation, reading up or checking on readiness and availability of equipment and manuals.

We had not achieved our ideal of no one in the client unit concerned knowing that this was only an exercise. We were not, therefore, testing the performance of those three who did know. However, given the structure of the client, we were never going to get our zero ideal and those that did know did not have crucial roles in the 'hands on' management of the crisis chosen. However, things would have been better if the General Manager had not been around and unruffled. In a rerun he would be removed from the unit and only available by telephone.

There was a need to restrain the crisis team from action that would bring matters into the public domain. This limited the range of people who could be contacted, but it was a useful constraint also – the 'need to know principle' applies to crises more than to much of business life.

The third major weakness was one inherent in all tests – the gaff might be blown. In this case we would revert to an open exercise, with increased time pressures, and we would still have had the advantage of running things blind for some of the period.

IMPLEMENTATION

Successful, we were not rumbled and we continued to the end. Actually, the exercise seemed so urgent and life-like that this consultancy's managing director said afterwards that at one point he began to believe in the illusion that mainly he had created and began to act out of role.

The commitment, contribution and general running round of people had meant that many more staff had become involved, if only in a peripheral way. It was, therefore, agreed to telescope all activities from 1.00 pm onwards to ensure that no staff would be going home believing the crisis to be continuing.

COMMENTARY AND LESSONS

Several things – most in fact – went according to plan, but the point of an exercise like this is to highlight what went wrong and learn from those problems. No action was taken that would have exacerbated matters but all was far too reactive to feel secure.

Crisis management team (CMT)

The team roles had traditionally been apportioned, as is commonplace and seems natural, correlating importance with seniority. Alternative staff in the absence of any team member – all positions need such substitutes – would, therefore, naturally be the next most junior. In any company, especially one predominantly involved in exporting, a certain percentage of senior management will be absent at any time. This produced a domino effect of almost no one acting in their prescribed and prepared roles. This did produce an amount of uncertainty and conflict of roles, where a staff member 'bumped out' of their expected role knew more than the person replacing them. Revision has since occurred to take into account those most likely to be away from the site, both in roles ascribed and substitutes chosen.

Invocation

As suspected, and for the reasons expected, there was a delay in invoking the crisis management procedure which resulted in time lost and energies misdirected away from the prime task of minimising the effect of the crisis. This has resulted in the introduction of an 'amber' stage of alert that people feel more able to invoke, and the redescription of the programme as 'damage limitation' which does not require the acknowledgement of the existence of a crisis for the process to begin.

Systems and equipment

Although things worked well in general, unexpected hiccoughs did arise. The telephone recording mechanism was too cumbersome, there was a need for more secure telephones away from the incident room so that handling could proceed without disruption, promises to the press to call back were overridden, confusion crept in when switchboard personnel changed over and so on. All are correctable and all are best revealed in a dummy run. Accurate logs and recordings were kept and were even intelligible.

CMT performance

The delay in invocation has already been noted. Strategic forward planning for possible developments tended to take a back seat to mechanical reaction. The original team structure had a place for such activity but this may well have been one of the casualties of the 'bumping up' of substitutes into uncharted positions – there was a element of the supposed strategic thinkers having expected to be mechanical doers.

The parent multinational, of course, had great resources that could be drawn on if contacted. They were not, and while this could in part be put down to the need to keep those in the know to a minimum, it was probably also a by-product of reluctance to acknowledge one's own problems to others. It was an opportunity missed.

Other shortcomings included:

- failure to prepare statements for sister companies in the group and for distributors and agents (these groups are friends to be protected and not hostiles to be held off);
- departure from agreed scripts of press statements (this can be as much a sign of a weak statement as of a staff failure);
- duplication of effort on straightforward mechanicals like product tracing (there is a seductive tendency to opt for mechanical action rather than strategic pro-action);
- failure to keep staff informed and reassured (unnecessary worry does not produce the best of responses).

GENERAL CONCLUSIONS

The official report concluded that 'the unit's performance [was] adequate in most respects' and that the exercise 'has resulted in the correction of any shortfalls for the future'. Which all sounds rather like faint praise for the client and self-justification for my consultancy. In fact, of course, many vital, important and necessary lessons were learnt that enabled the client to cope successfully with all crises that subsequently hit it. If it seems unlikely that lightning will strike the same place twice, it may be of interest that a very similar crisis did hit the client eighteen months later. The crisis was that alcohol was being smuggled into a dry Arab state using the client's shipments. Not surprisingly, this particular threat to reputation was dealt with in an amazingly efficient manner.

None of this came in time to avoid the immediate resentment and anger quite naturally felt by staff who had put their all under great stress for a whole day defending their company and livelihoods. Senior management and the PR associates spent most of the evening defusing this in the local pub – as we had expected and planned to do. Planning is very much a part of avoiding crises.

William Comery BA, BSc, is a director of Sheldon Communications Ltd, specialising in corporate business-to-business public relations. A formal background in research and marketing communications prior to entering mainstream PR has resulted in his continued involvement in strategic planning and in special exercises in crisis planning such as the one described above.

21 THE ROLE OF CONSULTANTS

The questions of whether or not to use outside consultants and, if so, how extensive their role should be in an RRM programme is one which is frequently raised. As a consultant my own instant reaction is, of course, that outside consultancies provide an indispensable service and should be employed on every aspect of RRM activity. There are, however, arguments for and against extensive use of consultancy services and considerations of how to make the most effective use of consultancy expertise.

CONSULTANT STRENGTHS

There are a number of clear benefits which an outside consultancy can bring to the creation and management of an RRM programme. The three most notable of these are breadth of experience, objectivity and capability. A major part of the work of a consultancy with RRM or crisis management capability will be to develop and support programmes for a variety of clients. This inevitably leads to a range of knowledge and direct experience of running such programmes which simply cannot be matched by 'in house' personnel. This experience will also include direct involvement in the management of crises on behalf of various clients at a level of frequency which could not occur within a single company.

A consultancy, other than one man operations, will also be able to draw on a level of combined experience from its executives which is unlikely to be matched in even the largest 'in house' departments. In a consultancy it is possible to assemble a team of experts for short periods when they are needed to deal with a particular issue. It is simply far too expensive for a company to meet the cost of keeping a similarly senior and qualified team permanently on the pay roll. For both these reasons it is extremely unlikely that any company will be able to come anywhere near matching the level of experience which is available from outside consultants.

The second major benefit which is offered by the outside consultant is objectivity and this can be valuable in more than one way. Because he or she is not a part of the day-to-day operation of a company's business it is much easier to stand back and gain a clear perspective of RRM needs – the cliché about not being able to see the wood for the trees really can apply. The consultant has a different, external perspective which applies to the general, social and commercial environment in which a company operates as well as to consideration of the specific activities and systems of the company. At every stage of RRM from risk assessment through to crisis management this perspective is helpful in setting priorities and identifying what is and what is not important.

Because he or she is not a part of a company's line management structure the outside consultant is not caught up in the multiple strands of different responsibilities and internal politics which are part and parcel of the work of any senior internal executive. This is a slightly different aspect of the consultant's objectivity to that of an external perspective but also has the effect of making it easier to focus on the key issues of the task in hand. It often also has the additional effect of providing greater access to senior personnel within an organisation, and of making it easier to gain Board level backing for proposed activity, although the latter of these is not necessarily a good thing. (It should not be the case that the views of an outside consultant are given more weight than would be given to precisely the same individual working within an organisation, but it very often is.)

The outside consultant is also likely to be more capable in dealing with reputation risk and crisis management than anyone working within a company. He or she will, quite crudely, probably be a lot better at the job. To some extent this higher level of capability is implicit in the benefit of greater levels of experience but it is rather more than this. For the internal executive, RRM is likely to be one part, possibly quite a small part, of his responsibilities but for the outside consultant it will be a primary part of his skill and a central part of his working life. Like any specialist he will have an immediate awareness of who, what, how and why, which is partly based on experience, partly based on day-to-day awareness, partly based on his skills being continually in use and, arguably, partly based on a natural aptitude for this fairly specialised field of consultancy. Of course, this rather strong claim will not always apply to specific individuals but for consultancies with a genuine capability and experience of RRM and crisis management it will virtually always be true.

CONSULTANT WEAKNESSES

While outside consultants are in a position to offer important benefits to an organisation there are also a number of considerations which may be seen to argue against their use or, at least, to argue for their role to be a limited one.

While objectivity can be a considerable advantage, the other side of the same coin is ignorance. The outside consultant will not, normally, have the same detailed knowledge of a company's operations, culture and, often unstated in any formal way, priorities. This is not, in itself, a fatal weakness and will frequently not matter at all, but it does mean that consultant views and recommendations have to be seen to lack that extra level of information.

Consultants are relatively expensive, normally charging on an hourly rate basis which is far higher than the comparable cost of 'in house' executive time – even when that time has been properly calculated to take into account the real cost of employees inclusive of all support service and overheads. This is true of any outside specialist – lawyers, accountants, all types of consultant – and does not mean that using such expertise is not desirable or cost effective. It does mean, however, that such time should be used intelligently. One does not expect to pay senior partner rates to a firm of accountants for running the payroll and, by the same token, one should not expect to pay top consultant rates for the more routine aspects of RRM. One should either do it oneself or negotiate different hourly rate levels to reflect the complexity and importance of the tasks which an outside consultancy is asked to take on board.

Experience and capability have been listed as two major benefits which outside consultants offer. This is not necessarily true of all companies claiming a 'crisis management' expertise. Crisis management has become a fashionable discipline and a serious money earner mainly for PR consultancies. As a consequence a large number of PR consultancies and others have developed a crisis management service for clients. Some of these are very good, but some are not. Rather too many 'experts' have emerged overnight in response to a perceived opportunity. It is well worth checking out the track record of firms providing an RRM or crisis management service to make sure that the personnel involved have genuine experience in the field and are not simply applying standard PR skills under a new name.

Protection of reputation is legitimately a PR responsibility and it is totally logical and proper that it is the PR industry which has developed particular expertise in RRM and crisis management. This single discipline approach does, however, carry the danger that the outside consultant may suffer from a degree of 'tunnel vision' in approaching the subject. Where one is looking to a consultancy to provide an 'across the board' service in RRM and crisis management it is as well to make sure that they are qualified to do this and have developed contacts and associate links, or have recruited staff with relevant expertise to ensure that they have a breadth of understanding and competence in handling the issues involved. Alternatively one needs to define an outside consultancy's terms of reference clearly and not expect particular expertise beyond its demonstrable area of capability.

STRIKING A BALANCE

In the final analysis it seems clear that it does make sense to involve outside, specialist expertise in developing and running an RRM programme and it makes sense to have access to such expertise fast if one is facing a crisis management problem. Provided that you select your consultancy carefully with a view to proven relevant experience and capability, the level of attention which will be devoted to your particular needs and charging levels; and provided you manage consultancy inputs with a view to cost effectiveness and areas of input, outside consultants will provide a level of expertise and knowledge which would not otherwise be available and will do so at a sensible level of cost.

At a very minimum it will make sense to draw on consultancy experience in setting up an RRM programme and to be able to access consultants for managing specific issues as they arise and, of course, for full blown crisis management. As a general rule consultant input to issue and crisis management will be more effective if there is a level of continuing involvement with the company. Such a relationship will normally prove far more effective than attempting to draw on consultancy help on an *ad hoc* basis. The level of this continuing input, which will normally be concerned with training and monitoring, is one which can only be determined on the basis of the specific circumstances and concerns of an organisation and can be very extensive or quite limited.

It is worth remembering that big is not necessarily best when choosing an outside consultancy; and it is not necessarily true that the most expensive provides the best service. It is a question of matching your own needs with skills and services which a consultancy offers and looking for an appropriate fit. At the same time, by and large, one gets what one pays for and attempting to buy in outside expertise on the cheap is normally a quick way of making a very poor bargain.

22 LAWYERS AND OTHER EXPERTS

There are a number of specialist advisers whose specific skills will be of value in planning and implementing activity which is designed to protect an organisation against risk. As a rule the skills which they bring to bear will be very specific to particular types of risk which a company may face either from external causes or from the consequences of its own actions. The one exception to this rule of specific responsibility is normally that of legal expertise which can be expected to have an input in a very wide range of RRM and crisis management activity.

In looking briefly at the types of specialist input which may be of value it will be sensible to take legal expertise last. It is a vexed question. On the one hand there can be no question that expert legal advice is crucial to a company managing potential or actual crisis. On the other hand there is a considerable weight of evidence to suggest that where companies act primarily on the basis of legal considerations in managing crisis the consequences are greatly against long term reputation interests.

SECURITY ADVISERS

A number of specialist firms and individual consultants offering particular expertise in all matters of security protection currently operate in Europe, the USA and the rest of the world's developed markets. Typically such firms draw on skills acquired from a background in law enforcement, the military, Government intelligence or private investigation. The services which they offer are largely related to prevention and pre-planning for particular types of risk and, depending on the nature of a company's business, can be extremely valuable. Areas where their inputs may be of particular value include:

- information protection against industrial espionage;
- personal protection/security for staff;

- protection and advice on consumer terrorism;
- industrial sabotage security;
- all physical protection and security systems.

The list is far from comprehensive and extends to security areas which do not relate directly to RRM or crisis management but which will be a part of a company's normal risk management activity. Although such services are mainly in the prevention area, they can also be used effectively in certain types of crisis e.g. kidnap of senior personnel, police interface on consumer blackmail threats etc.

The skills provided are not directly relevant to protection against reputation risk except in so far as they help demonstrate a company's competence in handling reputation threatening situations. However, the RRM manager will frequently want to work with such outside expertise and should be aware of what they can offer, and a familiarity with this aspect of risk and crisis management will be necessary for outside consultants employed primarily to help with information questions and reputation protection.

THE MONEY MEN

It would be a foolhardy executive indeed who chose to venture into the more complex aspects of the financial world without some training in the area or without clear guidance. The advice of accountants and company brokers is routinely taken as part of the normal management of a business and this advice is similarly valuable in RRM and crisis management.

The type of management crisis which is faced by a company combating a hostile takeover bid has not been dealt with in this book and it is not the intention to try to handle it here. It is a very special situation calling for very particular, City orientated skills and, although it may be perceived as a crisis for the Board which seeks to mount a defence, it is not normally a crisis of the type which threatens the future of a business, or the assets represented by that business' reputation. The relevance of RRM to such takeover situations is likely to be related to the continual programme of activity which ensures that a company's assets, tangible and intangible, are not under-valued and which makes the mounting of a hostile bid more difficult from the start.

Clearly the inputs of financial specialists are very important both in protecting a company's reputation within the financial community on a continuing basis and in handling crisis situations when they occur. Equally clearly such inputs will not be confined to the very special situation of the contested takeover but will relate to all financial aspects of company performance and to financial perceptions of a company. In the same way as with security advisers, however, the area where such expertise has major relevance to RRM is a limited one and it is important to keep it so.

Any worthwhile RRM manager and any competent consultant will be very aware of the financial community and of the company's shareholders as key publics. They will similarly be aware of potential consequences in the financial market of risks to corporate reputation. This does not mean, however, that the direct advice of financial experts should be taken as mainstream in all RRM decisions. The cost of a product recall is something a crisis management team may prefer to know before final authorisation but the issue will not be one of accounting; managing information flow in the wake of a disaster will require PR rather than brokerage skills even though the way this is done will have consequences in the City.

While financial advice is often vital it should be confined to its areas of relevance and where specific questions of reputation risk occur in the financial area it is well worth remembering that there are a number of specialist City PR firms whose skills in dealing with perceptions and attitudes within the financial community will, normally, be a great deal more finely tuned than those of the purely financial adviser. The City aspects of corporate and financial communications will usually be an element in management of reputation risk but it will not normally be the sole, or even the most important, aspect.

LAWYERS

Legal counsel is of a high order of importance in dealing with reputation risk and crisis management. It will be critical to a company facing risk to know what its legal position is, its responsibilities under the law and the legal consequences of any actions it may wish to take or statements it may wish to make. The role of 'corporate guru' which has been suggested for the core membership of the crisis management team will often be filled by a legal counsel and, when it is not, this member of the team must be able to draw on full legal advice to perform his or her role properly.

At the fundamental level of reputation risk assessment which underpins any fully managed RRM programme it will be necessary to know just what the legal position is on many identified risk areas and a knowledge of law will be valuable in identifying risk areas. Unlike the other two major areas of specific expertise, legal input is not confined to specific areas but has a potential relevance right across the field of risk areas in which a company may be involved, and herein lies a potential problem. The whole training and discipline of the law is one which is based on care and prudence, and very properly so. No matter that the courtroom performances of trial specialists make the headlines, or that the characters of 'LA Law' have become heroes in a super Soap. At base lawyers are predisposed to recommend a course of maximum circumspection and minimum exposure. In dealing with management of reputation risk or with crisis this approach may be appropriate, but often it is not. A position of 'I'm saying nothing until I see my lawyer' may be right for anyone being questioned by the police, whether innocent or guilty, but it is not the way in which one gains acceptance and sympathy in crisis management. Nor is it the way in which one can hope to seize the initiative in managing a potential or developing risk to reputation.

It is not the intention here to minimise the importance or relevance of legal inputs into the reputation risk management process. It is the intention to say that decisions which are taken on legal grounds alone, or which are over-influenced by the attitude of extreme caution which determines legal attitudes, will more often than not be wrong decisions. There is, in a crisis situation, a natural inclination to admit nothing, say nothing and attempt to control the crisis by drawing a protective wall of silence around the issue. Legal advice will tend to reinforce this inclination and most of the time this is positively *not* the way to manage a reputation risk, a threat to reputation nor, above all, a crisis. If one ignores the advice of lawyers as it pertains to the law then one is almost certainly making a mistake. But, simply because there are legal considerations in most reputation threatening situations, this does not mean that legal considerations are of paramount importance. Legal expertise needs to be given its due weight but no more than that.

EXPERTS IN GENERAL

We have looked at three types of expert, each with a role to play in RRM and crisis management. There are, of course, others though their role will tend to have a narrower range of application. Industrial relations, Government relations, insurance cover are some areas which spring immediately to mind.

When dealing with a crisis, and usually with reputation risk, it is neither practicable nor desirable to involve a whole range of experts in the decision making process. Their role has to be to provide information and advice, when it is called for. For particular issues which fall within a particular area of expertise one may wish to draft in an expert to help with decisions relating to that particular issue. Any attempt to canvass opinion on a wider basis, no matter how good the experts are in their own field, will rapidly result in a Tower of Babel effect and will hinder rather than help decision making. The two exceptions to this are legal counsel, whose input should be limited, and the RRM/crisis management expert, whose field of expertise is precisely the one which is of concern.

'AT THE COALFACE'
Crisis planning: common sense or defeatism?

Charles Griffith

Soon after I started work in a department of the British civil service, a heavy document thudded into the department. Created by a glory-seeking administrator who had clearly grown bored with his normal work, it gave ponderous step-by-step guidance for action in the event of a hijacking incident at a major airport. The head of my department belonged to an older generation which rightly considered the saving of paper to be pretty much the highest function of government. He sent the document back with a comment that, once analysed in detail, it only said that anyone going to the scene of an emergency should carry a pencil and paper. To me, he added: 'It's a poor thing when this service no longer relies on the common sense of its officers'.

I do have a lot sympathy with him. The government service, in particular, seems to be clogged up with people who spend their time imagining the worst possible case, and preparing for it in back-breaking detail. We all need to imagine the worst from time to time, but the process can easily become infectious, stifling initiative and adventure; and the worst, when it happens, often comes in a form which could never have been predicted. Of course there are valuable lessons to be learned from the more sensational business catastrophes of the past decade. Many corporations have shot themselves in the foot by the simple inability to define and communicate to the public the ways in which they were trying to get on top of problems such as pollution or product contamination. From time to time, these 'how-not-to' cases can be studied with profit. But my plea is that planning for crises should itself be handled with great care. Like fire drills, over-training can be almost as bad as no training. Thinking that things will go wrong is often a way to make them go wrong.

Any planning must take account of the particular culture and style of a business. There is a fine line between encouraging people to be responsible and prudent on the one hand, and scaring them off any form of initiative on the other. My preferred strategy would be to hold training in crisis management at fairly long intervals, and to lock the procedures and drill-books up in a safe place during these intervals. Often, too, the thrust of training should be on the lines of: 'We really have no idea what kind of a crisis may hit this organisation one day. When it comes, you are going to have to use your own commonsense and powers of improvisation. What this training can do is to give you a little more confidence in presenting yourselves and the corporation to the outside world'.

There is one aspect of crisis preparation which does need to be stressed in almost every organisation, and for which constant training is not only permissible, but highly desirable. This is the aspect of communication with the press and media. Luckily, this form of training need not be negative or defeatist. All senior personnel of all large corporations now have to face the possibility that, one day, they will be in front of the camera or the reporter's notebook, presenting either good or bad news about their organisation. The only way to handle this with any real skill and confidence is to practise with professional advisers, and to role-play the interview in advance.

For a British corporation, the task of on-going training in media presentation is especially important. In Britain, we have the best and the worst media in the world: the best in terms of giving a fair hearing to a properly argued case, but the worst when it comes to fastening on anything that looks like evasion or stone-walling. The good news is that personnel can be helped, by training, to work with the media and to use the media to give their company's point of view when things start to go seriously wrong. The bad news is that, if they are untrained and unsure of themselves in a crisis situation, they will make the situation worse for their company by almost every word they say; the hunted looks and stumbling words of so many oil company executives, caught in the spotlight of media attention after a particularly nasty oil-spill, are an awful warning here.

I stress again that training in dealing with the media is not just of value when a crisis breaks out. It is, or should be, part of a conscious and permanent policy of making the corporation more open about its general approach to social/consumer/community issues. Consumers and the general public are now demanding this kind of openness as a matter of course, and react badly to companies which do not take the trouble to present themselves on a day-to-day basis. This reaction will of course be especially strong if a major crisis does break out, but even if there never is such a traumatic event, the corporation will still benefit from a confident and relaxed relationship with the media.

Another aspect of corporate policy which can help in the event of a major crisis is the development of concise mission statements for the corporation as a whole, or for the individual divisions of the corporation. The concept of the 'mission statement' has sometimes been derided on the more cynical British side of the Atlantic, but I am convinced that it helps to sharpen and improve responses when, under the impact of a contamination scare or an environmental disaster, personnel are suddenly forced to improvise. As a great British General once put it, 'loneliness is the dominant emotion on the battlefield' – and, in my experience, an organisation reeling under an unforeseen emergency, has a lot in common with a military exercise. We all benefit, when things start exploding around us, from a clear idea in the back of our brains as to what we are supposed to be doing. Short encapsulations of the company's attitude to the community in which it lives can, perhaps, make a senior manager or director that much more confident under the glare of the camera.

Charles Griffith is an independent adviser on business and marketing communications strategies acting for multi-national companies and governments and with particular involvement in 'areas of opportunity' such as Eastern Europe and the Middle East. His particular areas of specialisation and previous background in government service provide him with an individual perspective on questions of reputation risk.

23 ADVERTISING

A major weapon in the communicator's armoury, advertising is, surprisingly, of limited value in handling the problems of reputation risk. There are a number of reasons for this.

- Advertising is, by definition, a means of reaching a wide public with one's message and can only be targeted in a very general way. Consequently it cannot be used in cases where one wishes to confine discussion with a limited interest group and has the direct effect of putting anything one wishes to say into the public domain. It is, therefore, unlikely to be an appropriate communications technique to employ at any stage of RRM prior to that of crisis management.
- There is a built-in suspicion of advertising claims amongst the general public (as evidenced by numerous surveys into consumer credibility in relation to advertising claims). This is not a serious problem when making product or corporate claims of an essentially selling nature, but does become so when trying to set out a clear statement of facts where one is seeking a 100 per cent acceptance of what is being said. Essentially, editorial coverage carries a far higher level of acceptance than any advertising claim.
- As a general rule advertising lends itself much more effectively to communicating relatively simple messages than to more complicated discussion of an issue (although this is not invariably true for specific ads) and in RRM the issues are rarely simple.
- In practice, the effect of advertising is frequently to draw additional attention to the issue involved and raise the profile of the problem being faced – much of the time RRM is concerned with damping down debate rather than encouraging it.
- Great care needs to be taken to ensure that the effect of an advertising campaign is not to produce a reaction which is precisely the opposite of the one intended. 'Methinks the gentleman protests too much' is an easily

provoked response from a largely cynical public considering a sensitive issue.

Having noted all of these limitations to advertising as a technique, however, it is clear that it also has some very definite benefits.

- The advertiser has total control over what is said in the advertisement and can set out his message without fear of it being garbled, modified or commented on by intermediate stages in the chain of communication.
- The advertiser can choose precisely where and when the message appears.
- Given a sufficiently large budget the advertiser can dominate a debate by sheer weight of coverage – roughly equivalent to shouting down an opponent in argument, and frequently an effective, if crude, technique.

For the RRM manager, then, advertising will often be a strategy of last resort. Potentially very powerful, but with the danger that it will backfire, it is normally only valuable once the issue involved has already entered the public domain and can be reasonably described as having reached a crisis stage.

One instance in which advertising may be absolutely necessary is when there is false information circulating about a company or its products. This is a situation which is almost impossible to address head on simply because it is a matter of false perceptions that have never become a matter of public debate. This was the sort of problem faced by the fast food chain McDonalds when it became a widely held belief that the company sourced beef from South American cattle grown in cleared areas of the rain forest and also that the company's packaging was produced using ozone threatening of gasses. Neither of these beliefs was true and neither was formally reported as being so, but rumour grew. In these circumstances part of McDonald's efforts to set the record straight involved advertising. This was, however, a very particular case.

It is always worth reminding oneself that the aim of RRM is to avoid and eliminate risks to reputation that may develop into crisis and, in the event of the unavoided crisis, to ensure that damage is kept to a minimum. This will always involve damping down the fires of debate, and even where proactive techniques are adopted, it will be with the clear intention of taking control of a situation in order to keep debate within bounds. It is rare for the best way of achieving this to be through mounting an advertising campaign.

It may seem somewhat cavalier to dismiss the power of advertising as being a secondary level technique in the management of reputation risk. It is, after all, the main way in which most companies communicate with their publics and is a prime way in which to build the reputations of corporations and of brands. The very size of the advertising industry testifies to the importance and value of this means of communication within the free market. However, when it comes to protecting those reputations against risk, its role is usually very limited.

In the context of RRM, the value of advertising usually lies in rebuilding reputation after the unavoided crisis has been survived. At this stage considerations of corporate reputation and straightforward marketing communications (rather than of RRM) will tend to dictate what approach should be taken, though it would be foolish indeed not to ensure an input from RRM into whatever advertising is planned.

24 THE CULPABLE COMPANY

Sometimes reputation risk develops into threat or crisis for reasons which are in no way the fault of the business which is placed at threat – terrorist activity, natural disaster, political developments, criminal product tampering, etc. Just as often the threat to a company's reputation is, at least partially, a result of action or failure to act on the part of the company or its employees. Whether or not a company has any direct responsibility for the situation in which it finds itself there will always be those who are quick to look for reasons to allocate blame, and where there has been death or injury this is a very human, if not wholly rational reaction. As has been said before, perceptions of a company faced with a crisis, or major threat to reputation will depend on three things:

- How far the company is perceived to have taken full and reasonable precautions to guard against the circumstances which threaten it, i.e. how culpable is the company?
- How effective has the company been in reacting to and minimising the damage caused?
- How far is the company seen to be genuinely concerned about what has happened at a level beyond that of purely business considerations, i.e. how human is the face of the company?

Managing these perceptions where a company has behaved properly and ethically is, we have argued, largely a matter of the proper and efficient management of information flow from the company. This is true even where a company may be held at least partly responsible for the situation which has arisen, provided that it can be shown that precautions had been taken even though they failed, that the situation was reacted to efficiently and that the company cared.

The position is a lot less clear and a lot less easy to manage where a company may be seen as being primarily to blame for the circumstances which threaten its reputation. It would be naive and unrealistic to pretend that every time a company faces a reputation threatening situation it is because of malevolent external influences, bad luck or explicable human error. The plain fact is that a significant number of corporate crises or even reputation threats are directly triggered by the conduct of the businesses, or the employees of those businesses. Where a company faces a threat to reputation as a result of its own culpability it is likely that it will immediately find itself dealing with crisis rather than reputation risk management. It may be that such crisis can be contained within limits and it may be on a comparatively small scale but it will not normally be a matter of day-to-day management of reputation risk. There are a number of reasons why this should be the case:

- Where a company can be seen to be culpable then there will be strong attribution of blame and where there is attribution of blame then there is little opportunity to defuse a situation prior to crisis mode.
- It is normally only possible for a company to carry on activity which would make it culpable in the event of something going wrong if that activity is unknown to relevant publics outside the company. For such activity, which may cover anything from poor hygiene or safety practice through to illegal activity by the company or its employees, to become a threat to reputation it must have become known beyond the company. This will usually mean that something has gone wrong and threat has already moved to crisis.
- Where an RRM programme has been put in place then reputation threatening practices will have been eliminated; or a conscious decision will have been taken to continue such practices and risk the consequences; or the risk assessment programme will have failed to identify the risk. If a conscious decision to continue has been taken, then it will only be when outside pressures force the company to address the issue that the company will be prepared for the issue to be raised at all, i.e. in a crisis. If the risk has not previously been identified then, again, it will only surface as a result of outside pressure or something going wrong and, again, one will already be dealing with some level of crisis.

There are exceptions to this rule such as cigarette manufacturers where there is indisputable evidence that these companies manufacture and sell a product which contributes to massive levels of ill-health and premature death. If such companies are not to be held culpable for the effects of smoking on health then it is difficult to know what the word 'culpable' means. Yet such companies are not facing crisis in the usual sense of the term unless one argues that, for the last ten years or so, they have been involved in a continuous and protracted form of crisis management.

In general, however, a company which is itself responsible for the actions which threaten to bring it into disrepute will have to deal with this threat in a crisis mode – the options of eliminating risk, deflecting a developing threat at an early stage or managing attitudinal change over a reasonable period are not open.

What, if anything, can be done to limit damage to reputation in such circumstances?

In fact a great deal can be done and, as in every instance of crisis management, the effectiveness of action will depend on recapturing the initiative and successfully influencing perceptions of a company to ensure that the most positive possible impressions are formed. A great deal of the success which a company achieves in protecting its reputation from the effects of a crisis for which it has itself been at least partly responsible will depend upon the strategy followed and the position which it decides to adopt. This is, of course, true of reputation protection in all cases of crisis management, but it is particularly true where there is genuine culpability and where there is a consequently greater need to influence the way in which events are interpreted. There are a number of choices of attitude and positioning which a company may adopt in these circumstances, some of which are worth looking at in fairly general terms.

The company as victim

Where it is possible to separate the company as an entity from the actions of some of its employees, or from a subsidiary aspect of its operations, it may be possible to present the company as the victim rather than the villain of a particular crisis. One has seen this achieved successfully by financial institutions which have been able to dissociate themselves from illegal or dubious trading activity by members of their staff, or where large organisations have effectively disowned the actions of a subsidiary company.

Positioning a company as being a victim in a crisis is, of course, fairly standard and is frequently an accurate reflection of what has happened. Switching perceptions from villain to victim is trickier but is certainly achievable in some circumstances. In order to do this successfully it is necessary to do more than simply point the finger of blame at some isolatable aspect of the company's operation. A company must also be seen to be doing everything to right whatever wrongs have been done, to be genuinely concerned and, above all, must communicate these attitudes quickly and effectively.

Showing that a company has itself been damaged by events, will guard against any future occurrence, cares deeply and shares a feeling of aggrievement with anyone who has been hurt can be an effective way of changing perceptions about degree of blame and can help corporate reputation to emerge from the crisis relatively intact. It should not be assumed that such a positioning is a dishonest one. Companies can be badly damaged by the actions of employees or by groups of employees which are totally counter to central management policy. Honest or dishonest, however, it will be perceptions not truth which will dictate the effect on reputation.

The penitent company

A variation on the company as victim positioning is the penitent company. Here a company admits to a failure in the past to live up to its own high standards but makes it clear that it has seen the error of its ways and will do better in the future. This type of approach may be extremely effective where a company has not suffered any type of disaster or major exposure of illegal business but where some aspect of its activity has been targeted as unacceptable by a powerful special interest group. There is, it should be said, a fair degree of divergence between business legality and public morality and a company may be acting perfectly legally, even ethically in business terms, and yet find itself facing a crisis of reputation when this practice is exposed to the public gaze. It is this public gaze which creates the crisis.

In some circumstances repudiation of previous business practice, clear statement of plans for change and a demonstration of sympathy with the views which have caused this change can actually enhance a company's reputation in the longer term.

The company in the wider debate

In some cases a company faces very serious reputation risk because a particular aspect of its products or business practices has been focused on and found wanting in some respect. In these circumstances it may be possible to widen the debate in such a way that this damaging focus is effectively blurred and is placed in a much more general context. This technique is normally only effective where crisis management is extended over a protracted period – crisis management normally starts fast, but can extend for a peculiarly long time.

Much of the time issues of this type are not simple matters of right or wrong but are genuinely complicated. There are some well publicised examples of this broadening of issues which initially appeared to pose a major threat to businesses in total, never mind reputation. The debate on cigarettes has been moved to some extent away from just how dangerous they are, and whether it should be legal to sell a lethal product, towards one of freedom of choice for people in a free society. The recent furore over the safety of breast implants in the UK, though not in the USA, has moved from the question of inadequate testing and clinical trials and on to a more general discussion of benefits to women, particularly after a mastectomy, and acceptable risk levels. The threat to boycott one major food producer's products because of allegedly unethical marketing of milk powder for babies in the Third World which became a major issue in the UK petered out in the face of a discussion which showed just how complex the issues surrounding product distribution to needy peoples can be.

Placing issues in a wider context as a means of defusing specific and focused attacks on a company's reputation is a fairly long term policy, but for a company which faces a reputation threat and which wishes to continue to carry on its business without significant change to either products or practices it may prove to be an effective long term method for managing that threat.

Admit nothing, say nothing

As a tactic for handling reputation risk in a crisis it is difficult to think of a worse approach than refusing to comment. There will be an automatic presumption of guilt, a complete failure to gain any sort of public sympathy and no opportunity to demonstrate that the company is reacting positively to the situation in which it finds itself. There are only two circumstances in which such an approach might possibly be justified. The first is where there is nothing which can conceivably be done which will not make matters worse, possibly because only some of the facts have come out and one is praying desperately that one can keep the full story out of the public eye – in general a forlorn hope. The second is where other considerations outweigh any reputation risk which may be faced, and this can happen.

For example, where a company is likely to be faced with massive claims for damages it may be that initial policy has to be to say as little as possible and to do absolutely nothing without legal advice. In the longer term one will wish to retake the initiative and set out the company position both to protect and rebuild corporate reputation and as part of the PR operation which will surround damage claims on a major scale, but in the short term a culpable company will not wish to provide any further ammunition which may be used against it. Even in these cases, however, it will make a great deal more sense for a company to stay non-commital on issues which it does not wish to discuss while still presenting as open an impression as it possibly can.

STRATEGY FOR SURVIVAL

There will be other positionings which can be considered and variations on the four approaches discussed here. What will be common to all approaches, if they are to be effective, is that they will have the long term aim of ensuring the survival of the company with as little damage done to it as possible. In practice crisis management may feel like a matter of survival but usually it is not – it is a matter of damage limitation and eventually business and reputation will recover. Successful crisis management will limit damage done and speed recovery. The fact that a company may be culpable is, no doubt, deplorable but does not alter the fact that the executives of such a company continue to have a duty to investors and employees alike to protect the company to the greatest degree possible. In order to achieve this it will be a critical part of long term strategy to minimise perceptions of corporate culpability while demonstrating ability to minimise damage done, and to do both in a way which presents the company in a sympathetic way.

If all of this seems over cynical it is not intended to be. Companies suffer major damage from crises which are not of their own making in any way, from crises which are only partially their responsibility and from crises which result primarily from their own failures. We have already discussed the priorities which should apply in managing a crisis and made it clear that the protection of a company's reputation should not be the *first* consideration but it should be *a* consideration.

No matter how a crisis may have been caused in the first place, the question of how to manage the reputation threatening aspects of that crisis is one of practicalities and not one of morals.

25 RRM AS THE COMPANY CONSCIENCE

We have looked at the processes of RRM as a defensive discipline and equated it with other forms of risk management. The thrust of the argument throughout has been that reputation has value and that this value should be protected by whatever means are available.

In doing this there has been an underlying assumption that, although a business may have been responsible for the reputation risks which it faces, the application of reputation risk and crisis management techniques cease to be appropriate when one is dealing with a business which has acted illegally or immorally as a fundamental part of its business practices and corporate culture.

This is, I believe, a reasonable assumption to make since when one is dealing with a completely unjustifiable situation which permeates an entire organisation it can no longer be a question of explanation and persuasion nor of justification, but rather of misdirection and concealment. There are, of course, techniques which may be employed to misdirect, conceal and distort issues. The most blatant of these is called 'lying'. More subtly it may be a matter of seeking to suppress information, discourage interest and of trying to direct enquiries towards different, safer aspects of a company's operations. The great weakness of such an approach is that when it fails to work it leaves a company in deeper trouble than when it started – and, in general, such an approach will fail to work.

The fact that a company may be seen to be culpable in a situation which threatens its reputation should not be equated with fundamental dishonesty or immorality. Companies do not deliberately seek to sell contaminated product by having slack quality control systems, cause accidents through poor safety precautions, employ deliberately dishonest executives, nor to do any of a range of things which might make them culpable in a crisis situation. There is a world of difference between falling short of ideal standards and the deliberate implementation of unethical business practices. Culpable companies should not resort to lies and evasions to protect their reputations and their businesses and when they do it is invariably a mistake. Criminal companies have little choice in the matter.

Unfortunately life is not as simple as the high moral tone of the last few paragraphs seems to suggest. Outside the schools of philosophy or the writings of theologians morality is something of a moveable feast. What is and is not legal not only changes through time and location but is a catch all concept covering everything from parking on a double yellow line through to mass murder. It would, I suspect, be impossible to find any company of substance where every action which is carried out conforms to a strict definition of legality and where nothing which is done could be criticised from at least some moral standpoint. What might have been regarded as acceptable business practice yesterday may well not be seen in the same light today and *vice versa*. In general there is a tendency for the general public, and specific key publics, to demand an ever greater moral accountability from business. Environmental issues, financial accountability, human rights issues have all become significantly more high profile over the past few decades, at least in the developed economies, but it is not a one way street. Greater religious, political and, in some respects, sexual tolerance has reduced other potential reputation risk areas over a similar period.

These are just a few of the ways in which perceptions of what is and is not ethically acceptable behaviour have changed, but whatever the prevailing fashions in moral and social values, it is a safe bet that there will be a degree of divergence between business ethics and publicly held social attitudes. How could it be otherwise? The considerations and objectives which determine an individual business' priorities are different from those which determine general social attitudes. This does not mean that there is a necessary conflict or that businesses are by definition antisocial. It does not mean that there will not be a great deal of common ground between business ethics and public ethics – on the contrary they will usually be identical in most respects. There will, however, be some divergence because the interests of the public and the interests of business are not identical – nor are their values.

There is a model of the way in which scientific revolutions occur, such as the change in belief that burning is caused by substances giving off a gas called 'phlogiston' to the belief that it is caused by combination with oxygen; or the change from a Newtonian to an Eisteinian view of the laws of physics. This model, put forward by Thomas Khun, says that there is what he describes as a 'paradigm shift' in thinking at a point when a sufficient level of evidence has piled up to refute one theory and to confirm another. This means that the shift to acceptance of a new theory is relatively rapid although not based on any single, convincing piece of evidence and, inevitably, there will be some scientists who cling on to the old theory even after the new has become the conventional wisdom of the world of science.

There is considerable support for the view that social attitudes change in much the same way. For example the adoption of 'green' values as the conventional wisdom of public and Governments alike has been a fairly rapid one. Concern for the environment moved from being a fringe issue to centre stage over a period of well under a decade, although most of the evidence which finally stimulated this shift in opinion had been known for a great deal longer. Just as there will be scientists left behind espousing old theories when a Khunian shift occurs, so there will be those whose social values fail to make the comparatively rapid switch to a new perspective. Corporate entities are amongst those bodies least likely to be able to reorientate attitudes at the flick of a mental switch. Successful companies have an investment in existing attitudes and practices and find it difficult to change these except in direct response to market pressure or, sometimes, opportunity.

It is when corporate values and activity diverge too far from society's values and codes of acceptable behaviour that a company moves into an area of serious reputation risk. It is in these circumstances that RRM activity may be seen as having a role which goes beyond defensive positioning and protective action in safeguarding reputation. In effect RRM activity will, as one part of indicating reputation risks, also be identifying areas of company operation which have shown an unacceptable degree of divergence and, in a way, will act as the company conscience – not for any reasons of absolute morality but for good, practical business reasons of avoiding putting assets unnecessarily at risk.

This may all sound highly theoretical but in practice it is not. The case history provided by Simon Taylor in his piece 'Overseas Chickens Come Home To Roost' (between Chapters 8 and 9) is a straightforward account of this process in operation. Cases such as the boycott by some customers of Barclays Bank in the '70's because of its policies on investment in South Africa are examples of the process failing to operate.

Companies do not exist in a vacuum and it would be absurd to suggest that it is only through a process of assessing reputation risk that a company will be aware of the moral climate in which it operates. Marketing policy, product positioning and selling techniques are all reliant on information about key public attitudes and opinions. Senior executives of the company are also members of the public and subject to the same social influences. Companies cannot hope to achieve success without good knowledge of factors affecting their business including laws and attitudes.

There is a wealth of information available upon which business policies may be based. None the less divergence occurs and it particularly occurs where there is no obvious penalty in being out of step with current attitudes – the marketing man who misinterprets public attitudes to a type of product will not last very long but the plant manager who saves money by skimping on pollution control may well get congratulated, at least until something goes wrong.

It is in these, marginalised, areas that reputation risk assessment and RRM should be allowed to influence policy by indicating the size and importance of risks involved and it is in these areas that company activity is most likely, as much through omission as through intent, to have become out of step with what would generally be regarded as responsible and ethical behaviour. Whether acceptable standards of behaviour are a matter of social consensus or are based on some form of moral absolutes is unimportant in this context. The motivation of RRM in moving company policy towards conformity with such acceptable standards is similarly irrelevant. If good business practice is something to be desired and if good business practice consists of conforming to acceptable standards of behaviour then RRM operates as a force for good in a wicked world! It is far from being the whole of a corporate conscience but it does have the potential to be an important part of it.

26 PUTTING IT ALL TOGETHER

Any discussion of any well defined aspect of management will be blinkered. Simply by concentrating on the specific issues which concern that particular part of the management process and on the considerations and techniques relevant to handling those issues the discussion is distorted. It gives a disproportionate emphasis to one particular set of disciplines.

In many companies, particularly at middle management levels, this focus on one aspect of operations at the expense of others is also a characteristic of individual managers. Engineers know that sales staff are a necessary evil but regard them as lower forms of corporate being. Salesmen know that invoices have to be paid and finances managed but regard financial personnel as non-productive overheads to be tolerated but not admired. Finance people know that everything finally hangs on the bottom line and cannot understand the fiscal naivety of salesman and engineers alike.

Reputation risk management is a discipline which, if it is to be practised successfully, cuts across all these artificial barriers of particular management interest. An attitude of mind which recognises the value of reputation and the need to protect this value against risk is the first level of RRM. Where such an awareness has permeated the company culture then an important part of a company's defences is already in place.

The specific management responsibilities and the particular areas of concern which provide the basis for an RRM programme have been discussed throughout this book and are capable, I believe, of fairly clear demarcation. However, though responsibilities may be very clearly defined, they cannot be allowed to rest solely within one function of an organisation. Just as there needs to be a general awareness of RRM needs, so RRM must be managed from the perspective of an overall understanding of the range of issues and risk areas involved. An important part of such an overall perspective must be to see just where the whole process of RRM fits into the corporate scheme of things.

Inevitably the discussion which has been conducted throughout this book has tended to emphasise the critical need of RRM in any organisation and to suggest that it is a management responsibility of the very highest priority. Such a view is true only insofar as it is true that there may be critical times, not limited to crisis management, when the protection of reputation is a central issue. Most of the time, however, the practice of RRM is not the prime concern of a business. It is a prudent and valuable set of management disciplines which can have serious consequences if ignored. It contributes to the prime aims of a business which will normally be the generation of wealth and the creation of employment through the provision of products or services, but it is not such an aim in itself. Failure to recognise these limitations will make the discipline of RRM less valuable to a company than when it is seen from the perspective of overall corporate interests.

Where judgement is concerned, and, as we have seen, RRM requires a considerable amount of judgement, the best interests of a company are not well served by giving undue weighting to any particular aspect of the issues involved, and the wish to protect reputation should not be allowed to become an excessively inhibiting factor in taking business decisions. Where this is allowed to happen then RRM will, at first, act against business interests and, eventually, become discredited and ignored.

Where priorities of corporate responsibility are concerned, care for reputation should not be allowed to override considerations of corporate duty towards employees, business partners and the general public (as can happen, for example, when a company suppresses information damaging to its reputation and in doing so allows people to be placed at risk). When Johnson and Johnson had to deal with the Tylenol crisis, neither the reputation of the brand nor of the corporation was the first consideration. Protection and then reassurance of the public took priority over damage limitation activity to guard reputation and this responsible approach actually had the effect of preserving the company's reputation better than any purely self-protective action could have done.

None of these *caveats* is intended to suggest that RRM is, in any way, an unimportant discipline. Rather they are intended to suggest that maintaining a sense of perspective is an essential part of effective RRM.

The other way in which RRM must be conducted with a clear sense of perspective is that it must start from an awareness of the company in relation to the external world. The reputation of a company, its brands and its services, is not something which is internal to a company. It depends on relationships with a number of key publics. It is a peculiarity of asset reputation that it is created by a business and adds value to a business but it exists in the minds of people who are, for the main part, not part of the business.

The term 'reputation' has been used as something of a catch-all throughout this book to cover the accumulation of attitudes which are held by key publics towards a company, its products and its services. It is these attitudes which will determine how these key publics will react in a whole variety of ways which directly affect the company's well being. These range from decisions on whether or not to purchase goods and products through to how to react to planning applications; and from how large a line of credit to extend through to whether to buy, hold or sell stock in a company.

It is not only at times of crisis that reputation may be threatened by events. In practice there is a continuous process of fire fighting which operates in parallel with a company's efforts to build reputation. There are, however, two critical differences between building and protecting reputation. Normally reputations can only be created over time but can be diminished, even destroyed in a matter of days, even hours. In general, reputation cannot be built and sustained without a solid support of real achievement. (Advertising may sell a product once but it is the quality of the product itself which will turn first sales into a strong franchise.) Reputations can, however, be damaged by perceptions which may be only very loosely based on fact.

The degree to which perceptions rather than reality determine the extent to which reputation may be put at risk has been emphasised time and time again in this discussion, but the sheer scale of the discrepancy which may occur cannot be overstated. Again and again public reaction is out of all proportion to the events which have brought it about, and time and time again one is surprised by the comparatively low key reaction to events which one might have expected to have had much greater impact.

An awareness of just how damaging it can be when negative reaction to events starts to become disproportionate is a critical aspect of RRM, and once one is aware of how easily this can happen the value of investing in a fully operational RRM programme becomes immediately apparent. Attitudes tend to feed on themselves, to snowball and to develop an internal momentum of their own. The more this momentum is allowed to develop independently of any input from a company the harder it is to bring any effective influence to bear.

It is often argued that the first 24 hours of a crisis determine how a company will be perceived and what the effects of the crisis on the company will be. Such a view is, I believe, to pinpoint the vital time period far too late. It is action taken prior to crisis which will be really vital both in preventing crises from occurring at all and in ensuring that, in the event of the unavoided crisis, those vital first 24 hours are not lost in confusion and panic reaction. Companies which plan to avoid crises will be less likely to have to deal with them, and companies which have anticipated the requirements of the unavoidable crisis will manage it better when it does occur. This applies to every aspect of a company's operations and not simply to threats to reputation, but at the end of the day it will be damage to reputation which has the longest lasting effect on brand or corporate health. It is also true that it is reputation which may be most arbitrarily placed at risk by events, to no particular person's gain but to a business' great detriment.

Implementation of a full and thorough reputation risk management programme is the logical outcome of a measured consideration of the value of those assets which take the form of reputation, of the risks which such assets face and of the steps which can be taken to defend them against such risk. While it has already been argued that considerations of prudent reputation protection should not be allowed to exert an undue influence over business decisions, it is similarly true that they should not be given less than their due weight. Reputation assets are no less real because they are intangible. A short term financial gain or avoidance of a short term financial loss which is achieved at the expense of threatening one's long term reputation is very unlikely to prove to be good business sense.

The one, self indulgent, literary quote which I have allowed myself comes from 'Othello'.

'Who steals my purse steals trash; 'tis something, nothing
'Twas mine, 'tis his, and has been slave to thousands
But he that filches from me my good name
Robs me of that which not enriches him
And makes me poor indeed'

Shakespeare was not concerned with a discussion of business profit and the financial value of reputation. But his words may be appropriated as a reminder of just how important it may be to put in place systems to protect reputation against threat.

Today's business environment is a long way from the world of the Elizabethan theatre and damage to one's reputation is unlikely to result in the painful death suffered by Desdemona in Shakespeare's play. However, damage to reputation will result in heavy cost to a corporation and, in extreme cases, may mean the extinction of a company or a brand.

The processes of RRM discussed in this book do not offer a cast iron protective shield for reputation but they do offer the best defence available.

Investment of money and of time in implementing such systems is not insignificant but it is trivial when measured against the potential cost of failing to do so.

APPENDIX
Brand valuation –
not just an accounting issue

John Murphy
Chairman, Interbrand Group plc
First appeared in ADMAP, April 1990

Interest in brand names and trade marks is at an all time high. Only two or
three years ago brand and brand names were considered the exclusive
preserve of marketing experts, now, one is as likely to hear a mergers and
acquisitions specialist or a finance director discoursing on the subject of
brand names as a marketing specialist.

THE ROWNTREE TAKEOVER BATTLE

The bitter takeover battle for control of Rowntree, one of Britain's – and
Europe's – major producers of branded chocolate and confectionery pro-
ducts is widely acknowledged as contributing greatly to the current interest
in brands. In this instance two wealthy and powerful Swiss companies,
Jacobs Suchard and Nestlé, competed with one another for control of
Rowntree, with Nestlé eventually emerging the winner.

Immediately before the initial takeover bid, Rowntree had a stock-market
capitalisation of c.£1,000 million, and tangible net assets (i.e., stocks, cash,
investments, plant and machinery, freeholds, etc.) of some £300 million.
Eventually, after a hard-fought takeover battle, Nestlé won control of
Rowntree at a price of £2,500 million – some eight times the tangible net
assets of the business. The immediate result of this bid was to make investors
and analysts aware of the fact that companies like Rowntree, who possess
strong brands, own assets which are valuable and rare and which hitherto,
have been relatively unrecognised. A fundamental reappraisal of the worth
of brands and of brand-owning companies has followed.

The high premium which Nestlé was prepared to pay for Rowntree was undoubtedly due in part to the rivalry existing between Jacobs Suchard and Nestlé, and the desire of Nestlé not to be bettered by a smaller competitor. But it is also due to a canny recognition by both Swiss companies of the power of brands and their capacity for producing sustained income.

BRAND VALUATION ACTIVITY

The wider awareness of the importance and value of brands, partly brought about by the Rowntree takeover, has had a number of consequences. One is the decision by a number of major companies to include brand values in their balance sheets. However, the practice has antecedents which pre-date the Rowntree takeover battle.

In 1984 News Group, the Australian flagship company of Rupert Murdoch's worldwide publishing empire, included a valuation for 'publishing titles' in its balance sheet. Murdoch did this because the 'goodwill' element of publishing acquisitions – the difference between the value of the net assets and the price paid – can be enormous. Being an acquisitive company, the goodwill write-offs which it was being forced to take were ravaging his balance sheet. He knew well that much of the 'goodwill' he was buying comprised the publishing titles; he therefore placed a value on these and included this valuation in the balance sheet, this simple procedure restored his balance sheet, solved many of the problems of goodwill write offs, and dramatically reduced gearing. Indeed, without the balance sheet valuation of publishing titles it is unlikely that Murdoch would have been able to expand his business by acquisition, particularly in the US.

Reckitt & Colman, the major UK based branded goods company, with powerful brands in the toiletries, household products and foods sector, was faced with exactly the same problem in 1985, having acquired Airwick Industries from Ciba-Geigy. It capitalised the value of the Airwick brand, for if it had not done so its net assets would have been reduced considerably.

Next in line was Grand Metropolitan. This company acquired Heublein in 1987 and Heublein's main asset was the Smirnoff brand. In August 1988 Grand Met announced that a large part of the sum it paid for Heublein was attributable to the Smirnoff brand and it would therefore not write this off but, rather, would include acquired brands in its balance sheet at a sum of £588 million. Not until later in the year did observers realise that this move was a trailer to the massive $5.5 billion Pillsbury bid, successfully concluded in January 1990.

The News Group, Reckitt & Colman and Grand Met brand valuations, and other valuations in the publishing industry, went largely unremarked.

(Observers did not altogether realise that publishing titles are in fact brands.) However, what really put the cat among the accounting pigeons was the decision of Rank Hovis McDougall plc (RHM), Britain's major flour and foods company, to value all its brands, acquired and otherwise, and to place this valuation in its balance sheet. News of this valuation broke in late November 1988 and controversy has raged ever since.

Since RHM valued its brands many major UK quoted companies – including Guinness, United Biscuits, Cadbury-Schweppes and Lonrho – have included brand valuations in their balance sheets, though mainly for acquired brands only. Guinness, for example, included a £1.7 billion valuation of brands acquired in the previous four years. Many more companies have valued their brands, but not used the valuation for balance sheet purposes. Rather, they have been more concerned with brand management, strategy, brand licensing and with the valuation of brands for merger and acquisition purposes.

The phenomenon of brand valuation has also spread well beyond Britain and Australia. A US observer has remarked that 'getting to grips with the value of important tangibles such as brands is one of the major challenges for US businesses and accountants in the 1990s'. Japanese business too is taking an interest – overseas acquisitions by Japanese companies are increasingly in the branded goods field, where much of the acquired value is intangible. Japanese companies are as keen as any others to evaluate the worth of the intangible assets they are acquiring.

THE BRAND VALUATION CONTROVERSY

Although the applications for brand valuation have grown well beyond 'balance sheet repair' and now include mergers and acquisitions, brand management, brand licensing and fund raising the 'balance sheet/brand valuation' debate continues. However, the debate is not really about brands at all: it is about the role of accounting (how accounting should adapt to a changing business environment, especially one in which 'worth' often principally comprises intangible, rather than tangible, assets) and the role of the balance sheet. The brand valuation debate has, therefore, precipitated a close look at issues which, many observers believe, the accountancy profession has fudged for far too long.

In many respects, therefore, the argument is something of a technical, accounting side show. Whatever accountants decide about the balance sheet, brand owners are aware that their brands are valuable and important. Investors and predators share precisely the same view.

While the balance sheet debate has raged, brand valuation has, more quietly, been applied in a number of quite different areas:

1   In merger and acquisitions, particularly to identify and evaluate opportunities, but also in disposals.
2   In brand licensing, both internally and to third parties. (Internal brand licensing can be highly tax efficient.)
3   In fund raising, brands are increasingly being used as collateral on loans, as they are freely transferable assets with clear title confirmed by trade mark registration certificates. Brands are also starting to be the subject of sale and lease back arrangements which are also proving highly tax-efficient.
4   For brand management purposes. Brand evaluation and valuation techniques must necessarily be extremely methodical, highly analytical and very thorough. Such techniques analyse each brand's strengths and weaknesses and have proved to be a management tool of considerable importance and value, particularly in the areas of resource allocation, brand strategy development and performance tracking.

It seems certain that the major long term impact of brand valuation will be in these areas, rather than in the specialised areas of balance sheet repair.

BRAND VALUATION IN MERGERS AND ACQUISITIONS

Consumer products companies know that it normally takes many years to establish a successful branded product and that successful branded products have to cover the considerable cost of the majority of brands that fail. The investment required to establish a successful brand will have taken place over an extended period and will have been accounted for in a variety of ways – capitalised manufacturing plant, expended or deferred research and development, expensed advertising and management costs and so on – little of which will be separately identifiable in a company's accounts.

Until recently no attempt has been made in the mergers and acquisitions arena to revisit the issue of valuing intangibles. Stock markets and investment banks have been generally content to let any premium paid to net tangible assets fall into the nebulous accounting category of goodwill.

Changes in the perception and financial treatment of this premium to tangible assets have, however, started. This development has arisen for both conceptual and technical reasons. Conceptually, many firms have found it increasingly unacceptable for their balance sheets to show littler indication of the true value of the company. Technically, the erosion of balance sheets by the conventional requirement to write off goodwill on acquisitions has left some companies looking over-geared. In addition the current rules on good will accounting result in a peculiar anomaly: the more acquisitive a company is in the branded goods area (where it is axiomatic that the main asset one is buying is intangible) the more that company will be forced to take goodwill write-offs to reserves, thus depleting net assets. Taken to its extreme a company such as Grand Metropolitan may find that its highly successful acquisition policy results in a balance sheet which has no reserves at all, yet Grand Met owns one of the world's most powerful and valuable brand portfolios.

The change in the perception and financial treatment of brand values by companies active in mergers and acquisitions is well illustrated by the example of Rank Hovis McDougall. The background to this pioneering step is instructive. Goodman Fielder Wattie, the Australian foods group, acquired a 15 per cent stake in RHM in 1986 from S & W Berisford, and in 1988 bid for RHM on a prospective multiple of 15.5 times earnings. This bid was referred to the Monopolies and Mergers Commission, and eventually lapsed. However, following the referral of the bid to the Monopolies and Mergers Commission the predator was left with a hostile 29.9 per cent stake with observers keenly anticipating the next move. The publication of the independent brand valuation conducted for RHM by Interbrand led to a further concentration of interest on the importance of brands by stock markets, analysts and investment bankers.

The aggregate RHM's net tangible and intangible assets following the brand valuation amounted to £0.98 billion, against the £1.78 billion price tag of the Goodman Fielder Wattie bid. The brand valuation was clearly not intended therefore to represent the worth of the business on a takeover, so what was it intended to represent? The answer is found in the test of RHM's own 1988 accounts:

'(The brand valuation) recognises the value of the brands as they are currently used by the Group and does not take account of their future prospects or, indeed, their worth in the open market.'

RHM is not, of course, the only instance where brand valuation has been centre stage during a takeover. The concept of brand value has featured prominently in a significant number of takeovers in recent years (see Table A.1). Surprisingly, most of these takeovers required a large premium in

Table A.1 Recent brand acquisitions in the food and drinks sector

Purchaser	Company acquired	Some key brands acquired	Cost	Date
R. J. Reynolds	Nabisco	Ritz Crackers, Planters nuts	$4.93bn	June 1985
Guinness	Arthur Bell	Bell's Whisky	£365m	Aug 1985
Philip Morris	General Foods	Bird's Eye, Maxwell House, Sanka	$5.8bn	Sept 1985
Guinness	Distillers	Jonnie Walker, White Horse, Gordon's Gin, Pimms	£2.7bn	Apr 1986
Allied Lyons	Hiram Walker	Canadian Club Courvoisier Cognac	£400m	Sept 1986
Elders LXL	Courage	Courage beers	£1.4bn	Nov 1986
Hillsdown Holdings	Maple Leaf Mills	Sun Maid raisins, Monarch flour, Purity flour	$169bn	July 1987
Douew Egberts	Akzo Consumer Products Div.	Temana, Heidelberg, etc	$612bn	Sept 1987
Cadbury Schweppes	Chocolate Poulain	Poulain Chocolate	£94.3m	Dec 1987
Seagram	Martell	Martell Cognac	£525m	Feb 1988
United Biscuits	Ross Young	Ross foods, Young's seafoods	£335m	Feb 1988
Nestlé	Rowntree	Kit-Kat, Rolo, Quality Street	£2.5bn	Apr 1988
KKR	RJR Nabisco	Winston, Camel, Benson and Hedges, Nabisco	$25.3bn	Nov 1988

Table A.1 (continued)

Purchaser	Company acquired	Some key brands acquired	Cost	Date
Grand Metropolitan	Pillsbury	Pillsbury, Green Giant, Burger King	$5.23bn	Oct 1988
Rank Hovis McDougal	RJR Nabisco (Breakfast Cereals UK)	Shredded Wheat, Shreddies, Team	£80m	Nov 1988
Brent Walker	Whyte & Mackay	Whyte & Mackay	£180m	Nov 1988
Cadbury Schweppes	Bassett foods	Liquorice Allsorts, Jelly Babies, Dolly Mixtures	£63m	Feb 1989
Mitsubishi	Princes/Trex	Princes canned foods, Trex	£55m estimate	Feb 1989
Allied Lyons	Chateau Latour	Chateau Latour	£110m	Apr 1989
Hillsdown	Premier Brands	Typhoo Tea, Marvel, Chivers	£195m	May 1989
BSN	Nabicrisps	Jacobs, Smiths, Walkers	$2.5bn	June 1989
Pepisico	Smitpotate	Smiths, Walkers	$1.35bn	July 1989
Polly Peck	Del Monte (fresh fruit)	Del Monte	$875m	Aug 1989
Cadbury Schweppes	Trebor	Trebor mints, Refreshers Extra Strong mints	£110m	Sept 1989
Cadbury Schweppes	Crush International	Crush, Gini, Hires	$220m	Oct 1989

Source: Hill Samuel

order to secure victory. Surprisingly, because it might be reasonable to have expected the increasing number of takeovers in the food and drinks sector to have led stock markets to two conclusions:

1 A major restructuring of the global food and drink manufacturing industry was under way as companies attempted to achieve sufficient critical mass to compete effectively in an increasingly international market place.
2 A significant element, influencing the bid premium which a predator might be prepared to pay, was the perception of the value of the brand portfolio.

Furthermore, investors might reasonably have been expected to be alert to the potential for bid activity in the consumer goods sectors and for this to be reflected in the market capitalisations of those branded goods companies which, for one reason or another, were likely to be vulnerable.

There are, however, several reasons why stock markets have to date generally failed to reassess significantly the value of companies with brand portfolios. Firstly, an act of faith would be required to build into a share price a premium to reflect the possibility of a bid without having any indication of when or from whom the bid might come. Secondly, and probably more important, has been the absence, until recently, of any objective yardstick to measure the value of brands in the same way that a company's other owned assets are valued.

Even with the emergence of a yardstick in the form of an independent valuation undertaken by specialists, the fairly small number of companies to have disclosed details of brand valuations in their published accounts has generally done little more than put a corporate toe in the water, as they have valued (with the main exception of RHM) only recently acquired brands. On the basis of these, it is probably premature to draw any firm conclusions about whether or not brand valuations have influenced market capitalisations. What can be said, however, is that the increased prominence of brands in mergers and acquisitions means that the concept of a brand's value is now firmly embedded in the consciousness of investment bankers, investors and analysts.

WHY RHM VALUED ITS BRANDS

In 1988 RHM had sales of almost £1,700 million, profits of almost £160 million, 50 or so of the leading food brands in the British, Australian, New

Zealand and 'Pacific rim' markets, almost 40,000 employees (90 per cent in the UK), a stock market capitalisation of £1,400 million but net assets of only £265 million. The reason for the low net asset figure was principally that the company had recently acquired another major foods group and had taken a substantial goodwill write off.

In late 1988, even though the hostile GFW bid had lapsed, RHM decided to include a formal valuation of its brands on its balance sheet. Its argument were:

1 It prided a more realistic picture of shareholders' funds.
2 It helps solve the goodwill write-off problem. Recognising the value of brands separately at the time of acquisition reduces the amount of goodwill that must be written off either directly to reserves or by amortisation over a number of years. Immediate write-off has a detrimental effect on consolidated reserves and confuses the real value of the acquisition to the business whereas amortisation has a continuing adverse and unrealistic effect on future profits.
3 It allows better comparison between companies operating in similar markets or between companies with varying mixes of acquired and own developed brands. (RHM saw no reason why acquired brands should be treated differently from 'home grown' brands since both can be equally valuable as assets to the to the company.)
4 It could assist capital raising by reducing gearing ratios.
5 It could provide the basis for brands to be included as assets for Stock Exchange class test purposes.

The valuation attached to RHM's brands was £678 million and the effect was to transform RHM's balance sheet with net assets rising from £265 million (in 1987) to £979 million (in 1988). Within a matter of days RHM announced that it had purchased Nabisco's UK breakfast cereals interests (a move which would have been difficult without the brand valuation) and RHM's City image changed in few months from that of a conservative, possibly even timid, miller and baker to that of a bold, pragmatic and successful foods group.

POSSIBLE WAYS TO VALUE BRANDS

During their initial investigations RHM and Interbrand looked at various methods of valuation including the following:

1 Valuation based on the aggregate cost of all marketing, advertising and

research and development expenditure, devoted to the brand over a stipulated period.

2 Valuation based on the premium pricing of a branded product over a non-branded product.

3 Valuation at market value.

4 Valuation based on various consumer-related factors such as esteem, recognition or awareness.

5 Valuation based on future earnings potential discounted to present day values.

Each of the above methods was rejected due to serious inherent drawbacks.

1 If the value of a brand is a function of the cost of its development, failed brands may well be attributed high values. This method also ignores the current financial position of the brand and the legal aspects of protectability and registration.

2 The major benefits of branded products to manufactures often relate to security and stability of future demand and effective utilisation of assets rather than to premium pricing. A strong brand which the retailer must stock due to customer demand provides a platform for the sale of additional products. It should also be remembered that many branded products (for example, a Mars bar) have no generic equivalents. The value of a brand clearly cannot be determined by higher prices or margins alone.

3 Brands are not developed with the intention of trading in them, nor is there a ready market to determine such values. The market value of any asset will be the amount that a third party might reasonably pay for it. In the case of a brand, the market value may fluctuate widely depending on the identity and intended purpose of the interested party. Furthermore, the use of market value for balance sheet purposes is prohibited in Britain by the Companies Act.

4 A brand valuation based solely on consumer esteem or awareness factors would bear no relationship to commercial reality.

5 The determination of reliable forecast cash flows, future growth patterns and an appropriate discount rate is fraught with difficulty. Furthermore, for an asset to be capitalised on the balance sheet, the fundamental accounting concepts of prudence and consistency must be applied. Any method relying on predicting future cash flow patterns fails to meet the requirements.

The methodology used by RHM and Interbrand computes the value of a brand by the application of an earning multiple to brand profitability, an overwhelmingly important factor in determining valuation. However, to arrive at a balance sheet value it is not enough merely to apply a simple multiplier to post tax profits. Firstly, not all of the profitability of a brand can necessarily be applied to a valuation of that brand. A brand may be essentially a commodity product, or may derive much of its profitability from its distribution system. The elements of profitability which do not result from the brand's identity must be excluded. Secondly, the value may be materially affected by using a single, possibly unrepresentative year's profit. RHM used a three year weighted average post tax profit figure to achieve this.

BRAND STRENGTH

The determination of the multiple to be applied to brand profit is derived from an in depth assessment of brand strength. This required a detailed review of each brand, its positions, the market in which it operates, competition, past performance, future plans, risks to the brand etc. The brand strength is a composite of seven weighted factors, each of which is scored according to clearly established and consistent guidelines. These key factors are:

- **Leadership:** A brand which leads its market sector is a more stable and valuable property than a brand lower down the order.
- **Stability:** Long established brands which command consumer loyalty and have become part of the 'fabric' of their markets are particularly valuable.
- **Market:** Brands in markets such as food and drinks are intrinsically more valuable than brands in, for example, high tech or clothing areas, as these latter markets are more vulnerable to technological and fashion changes.
- **Internationality:** Brands which are international are inherently more valuable than national or regional brands.
- **Trend:** The overall long term trend of the brand is an important measure of its ability to remain contemporary and relevant to consumers and hence of its value.
- **Support:** Those brand names which have received consistent investment and focused support must be regarded as more valuable than those which have not. While the amount spent in supporting a brand is important the quality of this support is equally significant.
- **Protection:** A registered trade mark is a statutory monopoly in a name, device or in a combination of these two. Other protection may exist in

common law, at least in certain countries. The strength and breadth of the brand's protection is critical in assessing its worth.

The brand is scored for each of these factors according to different weighting and the resultant total, known as the 'brand strength score', is expressed as a percentage.

THE DETERMINATION OF THE MULTIPLE

The relationship between brand strength as shown by the brand strength score and the multiple of earnings to be applied may be expressed graphically as an S Curve. In fixing the multiples to be applied to the brand strength score the closest available analogy to the return from a national perfect brand is the return from a risk free investment.

However, the perfect brand does not operate in a risk free environment, and the return from a risk free investment is capital free whilst part of a brand's earnings result from the capital employed in producing the product. Allowances for these factors must be taken into account in determining the multiple to be applied for a brand operations in a real business environment. Thus the highest multiple that can be applied will be somewhat lower than that for a risk free investment, and may vary from business to business and industry to industry.

The price/earnings ratios of industries serving consumer goods sectors also provide an indicator of multiples that can reasonably be applied to brands for balance sheet purposes. Thus the multiples at the high end of the scale should be greater than the average P/E ratio of the sector in which the company operates; those at the low end of the scale will be below this ratio. In practice, the multiple which the Interbrand methodology attributes to a notional 'perfect brand' is 20 times average annual brand related earnings though the multiple attributed to an 'average' brand is substantially lower than this.

AMORTISATION

Generally brands have no fixed life and therefore RHM's capitalisation of brands has been made without any provision for amortisation. However, should a brand suffer a domination in value a provision for this reduction would be required. It may however be possible for any domination which arises to be offset by revaluation of surpluses on other brands. Where a brand clearly has a finite life (e.g. a licensed brand), amortisation would of course be necessary.

APPLICATION FOR BRAND EVALUATION

The initial impetus for brand evaluation has clearly been a desire by companies with weakened balance sheets, as a result of post-acquisition goodwill write-offs, to restore these balance sheets to a state which more sensibly and accurately reflects the underlying financial strengths of the company. In doing so, however, they have stimulated a controversy which the chairman of the Accounting Standards Committee has described as 'the major accounting controversy of the last twenty years'. Many accountants, both in industry and private practice, have welcomed the inclusion of brands on the balance sheet and the stimulus which the brands debate has given to the accounting profession to find a solution to the intangibles (or 'goodwill') problem. Others, however, especially those in the technical department of the major accounting firms, have viewed the brands debate with something close to horror. In the summer of 1989 the London Business School entered the fray when it was retained by the Institute of Chartered Accountants in England and Wales to investigate the issue of brands on the balance sheet. While the LBS report encourages brand accounting for management purposes it concludes that including brands on the balance sheet 'is potentially corrosive to the whole basis of financial reporting'.

There is no doubt that the LBS report has lent strong support to the 'anti-brands-on-the-balance-sheet' faction but those who support brands on the balance sheet show no signs whatever of conceding defeat, in fact the reverse. Coopers & Lybrand, for example, have attacked the conclusions of the London Business School in a most outspoken report.

While the accounting debates rage, a host of applications have been developed for brand valuation which has nothing to do with balance sheets. After all, once brands are specifically identified as valuable assets the management of those assets becomes much more critical. As brands are, for many companies, the engines of profitability, it is clear that companies will wish to understand brands and their performance better, will wish to establish brand values for licensing (both internal and external) and will also wish, when buying or selling brands or brand rich companies, to understand in detail the strengths and profitability of these brands.

Hitherto, companies have not understood their brands well and in only a minority of cases have companies employed any form of brand accounting. It seems likely that brand valuation, initially undertaken mainly for reasons of balance sheet repair, will result quite quickly in a major reappraisal of these assets and how they are accounted for and managed.

THE FUTURE

The inclusion of brands on the balance sheet will continue to be a subject of major debate, particularly over the next two to three years. It is quite possible that the Accounting Standards Committee will seek to restrict the practice only to acquired brands; it may even seek to outlaw it altogether. Users of accounts, however, are unlikely to stand by and allow a return to 19th Century accounting when only things you can see, count and kick are allowed on the balance sheet. Whatever, therefore, is the short term outcome in accounting terms of the current brands debate, in the medium to long term it will result in a fundamental reappraisal of current accounting practices, probably on an international basis.

The brands debate is also leading, perhaps most importantly, to a fundamental reappraisal of brand management techniques and of the brand system. It is clear that the principles of brand husbandry need to be much better understood; that information systems' relation to brands needs to be fundamentally overhauled in most cases; and that the role of the brand manager needs to be redefined and integrated into the organisation at a much more senior level than is normally the case at present.

INDEX